D1311587

MEGACHANGE

Economic Disruption,

Political Upheaval,

and Social Strife

in the 21st Century

MEGACHANGE

DARRELL M. WEST

BROOKINGS INSTITUTION PRESS
Washington, D.C.

The Brookings Institution is a private nonprofit organization devoted to research, education, and publication on important issues of domestic and foreign policy. Its principal purpose is to bring the highest quality independent research and analysis to bear on current and emerging policy problems. Interpretations or conclusions in Brookings publications should be understood to be solely those of the authors.

Library of Congress Cataloging-in-Publication data is available.
ISBN 978-0-8157-2921-1 (cloth : alk. paper)
ISBN 978-0-8157-2922-8 (ebook)

9 8 7 6 5 4 3 2 1

Typeset in ITC Legacy.

Composition by Elliott Beard.

To Claude Wasserstein
For her continuing efforts to understand the world

Contents

Contents

Contents

List of Figures and Tables

Acknowledgments

I want to thank Tom Mann, Jonathan Ladd, and John Felton for their helpful comments on earlier drafts of this book. They made a number of suggestions that improved the writing. I am grateful for their thoughtful reviews.

In addition, Hillary Schaub provided terrific research assistance on this project. She worked tirelessly compiling information for the book, while also maintaining a cheerful disposition. I appreciate all that she did on this project.

A number of individuals at the Brookings Institution Press deserve a special thank you. Valentina Kalk, the director of the press, was a great source of advice about the book. William Finan expedited the review process and made a number of useful suggestions. Janet Walker was very helpful in supervising the book production process. Elliott Beard designed and typeset the book. None of these individuals is responsible for the interpretations presented in this volume.

CHAPTER 1

Overcoming Presentism

*One trap is "presentism," the idea that whatever is
happening now will keep happening.*

—E. J. DIONNE

For many decades, foreign policy experts assumed that communism was entrenched in the Soviet Union and Eastern Europe. Those countries' leaders had built powerful authoritarian states that monitored citizens, punished dissidents, and kept their parties in power. A few academics thought these regimes had internal contradictions that would lead to their inexorable demise.[1] But those forecasters were seen as contrarians and not taken very seriously by mainstream opinion leaders. When the Berlin Wall fell in 1989 and the Soviet Union dissolved two years later, the internal politics and economies of nearly twenty European and Central Asian countries were transformed, disrupting political alignments around the world.

Top financial investors were shocked in 2008 when leading Wall Street firms collapsed and a Great Recession unfolded. Bear Stearns and Lehman Brothers closed their doors, stock markets around the world lost as much as half their value, and many banks stopped lending money. Following decades during which no one could conceive the possibility of another Great Depression, the world suddenly came perilously close to a global financial meltdown.[2] The devastating economic impact unleashed public anger against large financial institutions and governments, and aggravated the plight of the working class in many countries.

Most people in the Western world were caught off-guard in 2014 when a group of Muslim fighters calling themselves the Islamic State of Iraq and Syria (ISIS), declared a caliphate after taking control of large parts of Iraq and Syria.[3] Establishing a theocratic empire led by a single religious and political figure seemed medieval to much of the world, and ISIS leaders did little to dispel that impression when their followers publicly beheaded hostages and burned adversaries alive.[4] Observers around the world wondered how this kind of barbarism could exist during an era of globalization, secular cosmopolitanism, and extraordinary scientific progress.

In 2016 people in the United Kingdom confounded the experts by voting 52 to 48 percent to leave the European Union (EU). In the weeks leading up to the referendum, financial and diplomatic authorities had warned of dire consequences to fiscal stability, economic growth, and international trade if the exit were approved. But riding a wave of nationalist and anti-Brussels sentiment, voters supported withdrawal from the EU and an independent future for Great Britain. The move startled the EU bloc, led to a dramatic sell-off of the British pound, and rattled financial and political decisionmakers around the world.[5]

It is no accident that large-scale change is taking place in the contemporary period. Many of the beliefs and institutions that once anchored international and domestic affairs have grown weak. Political tidal waves have occurred in many parts of the world. We live in an era where major events occur on a seemingly regular basis.[6] *Megachange* refers to dramatic shifts in social, economic, or political phenomena. These alterations can include economic disruptions, political upheaval, or social strife, among other things. Any one of these can generate ramifications that go beyond the small-scale, incremental shifts that historically typified many societal developments. While the extent and pace of change today seems exceptionally dramatic, the current period is not the first to show evidence of large-scale change. Throughout history, empires and civilizations came and went with regularity. Nations rose in prominence and then collapsed due to economic challenges, foreign invasion, internal conflicts, or natural disasters. Dramatic scientific discoveries disrupted business practices, or new societal orders such as the Reformation and the Industrial Revolution fundamentally altered people's lives.

In more recent times, there also have been major shifts. For example, the United States faced substantial transformations in the 1860s during and after the Civil War, again in the 1930s due to the Great Depression, and in the 1960s with the rise of the civil rights, women's liberation, and environmental movements. In a relatively short time, large-scale disruptions altered society and politics and left a lasting imprint on those eras.

In various epochs, there have been significant fluctuations in public policies or citizen attitudes associated with social, political, or economic change. For example, following a period of social and religious turmoil, an American prohibition on the production and sale of alcohol was adopted nationally in 1920 and remained in effect until 1933. After women began organizing politically in the late 1800s, Western countries gradually adopted female suffrage, including the United States in 1920 through a constitutional amendment. Reflecting the shifting cultural mores of a later period, a dramatic 1973 U. S. Supreme Court decision legalized abortion across the country.[7]

It never is easy to disentangle causes and consequences of large-scale transformations. As I describe in this volume, change is chaotic and multifaceted and therefore hard to pin down precisely. One has to look over a period of time to see what is shifting and what forces are generating the most substantial alterations.

Yet through case studies, it is possible to elucidate the megachanges that have affected global affairs and American politics in recent decades. Domestically, we see megachange in shifting attitudes toward same-sex marriage, tobacco smoking, marijuana legalization, income inequality, terrorism, and border security. Globally, we have witnessed the rise and collapse of the "Arab Spring," the reemergence of religious zealotry, the violence of nonstate actors, and challenges to the open flow of people, goods, and services long associated with globalization.

Sometimes, what happens internationally influences domestic politics, or vice versa. Extremism in one locale can provoke tensions far from the original site. In an era of global communications and speedy information transmission, seemingly small events can reverberate elsewhere and become a catalyst for dramatic change in domestic or international affairs.

The term "quantum leap," borrowed from physicists, has come to popularly mean large-scale changes that leap-frog existing knowledge and introduce new ways of thinking. Philosophers talk about "paradigm shifts" where theoretical frameworks change dramatically. Biologists refer to models of "punctuated equilibrium" in which there is a time of great change followed by periods of equilibrium.[8] Digital experts emphasize "disruptive technology" that challenges old ways of doing things and leads to the rise of companies that take advantage of, or even help create, new market realities.[9]

Unusual developments also periodically take place in politics. As pointed out by commentator Jeff Greenfield, "There are times in politics when the Black Swan shows up; when a highly unlikely, highly improbable event shatters years' worth of assumptions."[10] Political earthquakes no longer seem very rare, as demonstrated by the unlikely emergence of Donald Trump in 2016.

In the area of economics, Tyler Cowen argues that "average is over."[11] Because of the great stagnation after 2008, he now believes it is going to be difficult to generate robust and sustained economic growth. The past is not prologue to the future. Rather, a number of factors will restrict prosperity unless substantial action is taken to reverse the current tide.

Extending that notion is a book by economist James K. Galbraith. He has written about the "end of normal." Analyzing macroeconomic performance, he says that people should not project economic growth from the 1950s through 2000 into the future. Many of the conditions that gave rise to strong performance have disappeared, and it is going to be difficult to maintain past trends in the near-future.[12]

Economist Robert Gordon argues that we are seeing a major change in growth patterns. In his recent volume, *The Rise and Fall of American Growth*, he claims the dramatic growth that marked the period from 1870 to 1970 has ended and there no longer are major advances in labor productivity or societal innovation. With an aging population and high inequality, the U.S. standard of living is likely to stagnate or even fall.[13]

Running through each of these notions is the idea that something big is happening in the current period. Social, economic, and political patterns no longer are fixed but are generating rapid and transformative shifts. People need to be prepared for a scope of change that is grander than typically envisioned. Until we better understand these tectonic movements, it will be difficult for individuals and societies as a whole to deal with their extraordinary impact.

Big Moves Abroad

Internationally, there are numerous signs of major developments and shifting alignments. For most of the past seven decades, strong international norms seemed to guarantee the sanctity of national borders. Given the widespread aggression leading up to and during World War II and the great loss of life that resulted, modern nations generally have refrained from foreign invasions. They do not want to risk international conflagrations and the high human costs that result. Global organizations make many efforts to discourage countries from violating sovereign rights of other countries—all in hopes of keeping the peace and maintaining friendly relations across the international order.

Yet that long-held norm is breaking down. Western leaders were unprepared in 2014 when Russia invaded and annexed Crimea and then moved into the eastern part of Ukraine with the stated goal of protecting Russian interests. Crimea had been ceded to Ukraine in 1954 by the Soviet Union and had become a vital part of that country. The peninsula on the Black Sea used Ukrainian currency and had representation in the national parliament.

Despite international condemnation of the annexation, Russia refused to reverse course. Western leaders used impassioned rhetoric against the takeover, imposed trade and banking sanctions on the invader, and increased aid to Ukraine. Yet for more than two years the world has not figured out how to change the on-ground reality. Few leaders wanted to send troops to counter what they considered blatant Russian aggression.

Along with its rapidly increasing economic power, China has become much more active in regional and global affairs, and it has imposed limits on foreign organizations and multinational corporations that operate within its borders. It has challenged Japanese sovereignty over the Senkaku Islands in the East China Sea. Although these spots have been controlled by Japan for a long period of time, China asserted its territorial rights after oil reserves were discovered. It said that its geographical prerogatives pre-date those of Japan. The Chinese military sent boats and planes to the region in order to protect its own geographic claims and has installed surface-to-air missiles on one disputed island.[14]

In addition, China has built seven artificial islands on reefs in the South China Sea and declared Chinese sovereignty over the twelve miles surrounding each construction.[15] This expansion in territorial claims has complicated U.S. military operations in the region and threatened the ability of some commercial ships to travel freely through those passages. These fears were heightened when China began installing long runways, military barracks, and missiles on the Paracel Islands. Neighboring countries—most of them U.S. allies and trading partners—worried that these moves were a sign of bald geopolitical ambitions on the part of China.[16]

In one encounter with an American military jet in the South China Sea, Chinese sailors sought to force the pilot away from the area. "Foreign military aircraft. This is Chinese navy. You are approaching our military alert zone. Leave immediately," the unnamed person warned.[17] Even though the plane was in international airspace, China claimed territorial rights in this encounter and sought to extend those rights to nearly 80 percent of the South China Sea. This put China in direct conflict with nations such as Vietnam, Malaysia, the Philippines, and Taiwan, all of which had sovereignty over parts of this waterway.

The Arab Spring uprisings caught nearly all governments and political commentators flat-footed. Most were surprised in 2010 when street protests erupted in Tunisia and sparked demonstrations in several Middle Eastern countries.[18] Grievances against incompetence and corruption by authoritarian regimes throughout the Arab world resonated with ordinary people, thousands of whom surged into the region's streets in an extraordinary series of protests. As they had done in other periods, governments moved to suppress the complaints and arrest protestors.

But the political movements toppled several authoritarian leaders who had seemed entrenched in power, notably President Hosni Mubarak in Egypt. Hardly any knowledgeable analyst anticipated the series of revolutions that quickly swept through North Africa and the Middle East. In short order, there were provisional governments in Tunisia, Libya, and Egypt. Syria and Yemen fell into devastating civil wars as rival factions jockeyed for political and economic power, and Libya has faced similar turmoil after the ouster and execution of Muammar Qaddafi.

Through these and other examples, I argue that many of the social, economic, and political forces that once constrained large-scale international change have grown weak. Old alignments have broken down and new ones are emerging—or in some cases new alignments are not even apparent as yet. Great power conflict, which seemed unimaginable in the nuclear era, has returned as a possible danger. The idea that nations would limit their territorial claims has given way to extensive jockeying among nations, testing geographic boundaries and violating traditional norms.

The post-1989 world order dominated by the United States has developed into one that now features an ascendant China, an aggressive Russia, and violent non-state actors such as the Islamic State of Iraq and Syria (ISIS), Al Qaeda, Al Shabaab, and Boko Haram. The latter groups apply strict religious laws to territories they control and employ primitive practices such as systematic rape, sexual slavery, and feudal governance.[19] Limits on Western power are apparent, and the ability of America and Europe to take effective action is seriously constrained.

In essence, the globe has moved from a bipolar world during

the Cold War, to a unipolar one following the collapse of the Soviet Union when the United States became the dominant power, and since 9/11 to a multipolar world reflecting the emergence of new powers and non-state actors. Bipolar and unipolar world orders generally are stable because of the dominance of a limited number of powers that often can control local and regional conflicts. However, the shift to multipolarity signals a rise in instability as various powers jockey for advantage and no single power (including China, Russia, Europe, or the United States) has the capacity to dictate outcomes.[20]

Some of the new global complexities reflect long-standing conflicts over natural resources, economic interests, or old-fashioned political rivalries. An intertwined world seems to have an increased number and intensity of disputes over trading practices, business relationships, or national policies. This destabilizes cross-country ties and generates social, economic, and political disputes.

Yet some of this turmoil reflects new sources of unpredictability. For example, there are failed states or ungoverned areas in many locales around the world.[21] A handful of places, especially in Africa and the Middle East, have governments that lack authority and are unable to limit aggressive behavior. Criminal networks and informal organizations have gained power and are able to control streets, neighborhoods, or even entire sections of countries. These networks affect both international relations and domestic politics, and they test the limits of conventional behavior.

Religious strife has entered an ominous phase as well. There has been an emergence of fundamentalism in each of the world's three monotheistic religions—Judaism, Islam, and Christianity—complicating geopolitics. As noted by Michael Walzer in his book *The Paradox of Liberation: Secular Revolutions and Religious Counterrevolutions*, an epic battle is taking place between the forces of modernity and secularization versus those who believe those forces are absolutely wrong.[22] Religious conflict takes a variety of forms in different locales, but disagreements regarding the role of women, homosexuality, and cultural permissiveness permeate many regional and global tensions.

Digital technology has complicated global politics by speeding up communications and altering traditional patterns of social and economic interaction.[23] Advances in communications make it easier than ever before for those who are dissatisfied to organize. What used to be local disputes can go viral and spread rapidly—even worldwide—through social media and digital technology. In an era of globalization, international communications channels have brought people of diverse backgrounds and interests into virtual but remarkably intimate contact with one another. Differences that previously could be papered over or even ignored now come into people's personal space and force them to think about natural disasters, political conflicts, or social turmoil thousands of miles away. The result often is an increase in anxiety, ill feelings, and global tensions.[24]

Disruptions at Home

It is not just global affairs that have become unsettled. In the same way that things have been in flux on the international scene, startling developments have roiled U.S. domestic politics during the past two decades. They include the impeachment but failed removal of a president (Bill Clinton), the 9/11 terrorist attacks, the Great Recession, the election of an African American chief executive (Barack Obama), a woman and a democratic socialist running for president (Hillary Clinton and Bernie Sanders, respectively), a populist billionaire seeking the top job (Donald Trump), and the death of a key justice (Antonin Scalia) on a sharply divided Supreme Court.

These events illustrate how much political turmoil there has been in recent years. In the post–World War II period, many observers viewed incrementalism as the best description of American politics.[25] This is the perspective that small-scale shifts and gradual evolution represent the norm, rather than revolution or large-scale developments. Because this idea seemed both to describe actual policy processes and the virtues of small-scale shifts, analysts touted it as the dominant paradigm of the last fifty years.[26] Change, it was argued, occurs slowly because many social, political, and institutional factors constrain large-scale transformation.

In at least the past two decades, though, domestic politics have become more extreme and more polarized—and as a result proposed solutions have become more radical in nature because negotiation and compromise no longer are fashionable. Some of the things that have destabilized the international order and broadened the range of possible actions also are apparent domestically. Large forces have shaken the social and political foundations of civil society and affected a wide range of areas.

Broad political developments such as the Reagan Revolution in 1980 placed the country on a more conservative policy course. The 1994 midterm elections accentuated that trend by putting Republicans in charge of the House of Representatives for the first time in forty years. After this outcome, the GOP would hold the House for eighteen of the following twenty-two years and use this power to attempt to downsize government and curtail social welfare programs.

However, the Great Recession upended GOP control, at least for a time. The United States elected its first African American president in 2008 and gave him big Democratic majorities in the House and Senate. He would use that advantage to enact comprehensive bills to stimulate the economy, regulate large financial institutions, and transform American health care.

Obama's success generated an intense backlash, however, enabling Republicans to again take control of Congress and thus stymie nearly all of his subsequent initiatives. These types of widespread swings in political power, leading to dramatic policy initiatives, no longer are unusual. As noted by John Piescik and his colleagues, comprehensive policymaking in large organizations is very much in vogue during the contemporary era.[27] During recent years, there have been major shifts in tax policy (large cuts for the wealthy under George W. Bush), financial regulation (the Dodd-Frank legislation under Obama), climate change (a historic agreement with China on reducing carbon emissions), and a hefty increase in income tax rates on the wealthy under Obama (as part of the "fiscal cliff" negotiations). Legislative efforts to adopt comprehensive immigration reform failed amidst partisan gridlock, but Obama responded by adopting major changes through an executive order, though he has been challenged in court.

As is the case globally, a variety of forces enable broad-based domestic change. There is a widely shared sense that things are floundering in the United States, and this creates an appetite across the political spectrum for more substantial actions. Rather than stick with small-bore measures, politicians of the left and right have advocated such widely divergent proposals as banning Muslims from entering the United States due to terrorism concerns, privatizing Social Security, abolishing the Internal Revenue Service, restructuring or even ditching the North Atlantic Treaty Organization (NATO), dropping out of international trade agreements, and providing free community college tuition for all students.

For much of American history, the nature of party coalitions discouraged radicalism and promoted bargaining, compromise, and negotiation. Old models talked about the "median voter" as the primary object of party competition. The idea was that public opinion resembled a bell-shaped curve with most people in the political center and smaller numbers on the left and right, respectively. In that situation, the winning political strategy was clear. Candidates should aim for the middle, propose moderate steps that seemed workable, and compromise with the other party to govern and pass legislation. Such a process slowed the pace of politics and made incrementalism an accurate description of policy change.

In recent years, though, fighting for centrist voters has given way to playing to the extreme base in both parties. With low voter turnout and polarized electorates, candidates have determined that it often makes more sense to mobilize left- or right-wing voters than play to the middle. Many candidates and party activists prefer "red meat" appeals that generate excitement rather than complex or nuanced proposals that reaffirm the status quo. Also, donors, who have become increasingly vital to the political process because of the enormous costs of campaigns, often have more extreme viewpoints than the electorate as a whole—and so they help push candidates to the far edges.

Figure 1-1 shows the percentage of Democrats and Republicans in the House of Representatives who had centrist voting records between 1951 and 2013. At the beginning of that period, nearly 60 percent of the representatives in each party tended to vote for "moderate" positions. By 2013, though, the number of moderate Democrats had fallen to 13 percent while those within the GOP almost completely disappeared.[28]

In Congress and many state legislatures, those who are willing to cross party lines and support bipartisan compromises are seen as traitors to the cause. That is especially the case among Republicans since the rise of the Tea Party in 2010. Conservatives outraged over fast-rising government debt and increased public spending, among other perceived ills, organized to "take back" the future and return to cherished values from the past. But the collapse of moderation also has taken

FIGURE 1-1. *Democrats and Republicans*
Who Are Moderate

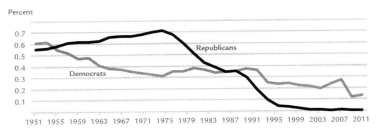

Source: Keith Poole, "The Polarization of the Congressional Parties," March 21, 2015.

place on the Democratic side, as demonstrated by the surprisingly strong support for socialist Bernie Sanders in the 2016 nominating process.

The result in both parties has been that politicians of many stripes have put forward proposals for radical change and strongly resisted proposals from the opposing side. Many legislators want to "think big" and produce dramatic shifts in public policy, encouraged by voters upset with their own diminished financial fortunes or motivated by their negative views of government.[29] Research has shown a strong tie between economic disruption and political extremism. An examination of congressional voting patterns and local job losses demonstrates that "areas hardest hit by trade shocks were much more likely to move to the far right or the far left politically."[30]

Changes in the news media furthermore have promoted major alterations in the political sphere. With only a few exceptions, the news media have fragmented into competing "echo chambers" that tell people what they want to hear, based on market research rather than serious journalistic values. Moreover, many individuals (especially young people) no longer rely upon the mainstream media for daily information. Instead, they get news, or what they perceive as news, through social media and digital platforms. The result is a media system that, too often, pushes people apart rather than brings them together. Public discourse ends up being based more on opinions than facts, and there is little agreement on the challenges facing the country.

Extremism Begets Extremism

In today's world, domestic and foreign policy interact in sometimes disturbing ways. People of the world no longer are isolated and cut off from distant lands. Through instant communication, they can see injustice and unfairness, whether it's committed on the other side of the planet or is directed at members of their own racial or ethnic group, gender, religious faith, or social class. Provocations in one place can set off political disturbances far from the original scene.

The emergence of the Internet has boosted access to information exponentially and made it easy to inflame tensions by disseminating false or misleading claims, as well as valid information. Similar to Gutenberg's invention of the printing press in 1440, digital technology has been profoundly disruptive of existing power relationships. By reducing publication costs through mass production, the printing press is said by sociologist Paul Starr to have sparked the Protestant Reformation, undermined the Catholic Church, intensified religious conflict, and played a role in several civil wars across Europe in the fifteenth and sixteenth centuries.[31]

Through modern-day technology, such as the Internet and social media, contemporary events can ripple around the globe and affect people's impressions. Many countries today contain a heterogeneous set of races, religions, ethnicities, and political viewpoints. Amidst this kaleidoscope of orientations, people in one place pay attention to how like-minded individuals are treated elsewhere. In this situation, it is easy to feel outrage over real or perceived injustice.

One egregious example of this occurred in the 2016 U.S. presidential campaign. After ISIS-inspired terrorists murdered fourteen innocent civilians in San Bernardino, California, in December 2015, Republican candidate Donald Trump argued that the United States should ban Muslims from entering the country (a claim he repeated after the Orlando mass killings at a gay nightclub). The East African terrorist organization Al Shabaab then used his exclusionary and intolerant rhetoric to recruit fighters on grounds that the United States was waging war on Islam.[32]

Following the March 2016 ISIS bombings in Brussels, that group made a video in which it used comments by the GOP billionaire to bolster its claims about the scale of the carnage. The video quoted Trump as saying: "Brussels was one of the great cities—one of the most beautiful cities of the world 20 years ago—and safe. And now it's a horror show—an absolute horror show."[33]

On the CBS television show *Face the Nation*, moderator John Dickerson asked Trump about his provocative stance on Muslims. The presidential candidate responded by saying the United States had grown weak and was placing unreasonable restrictions on military operations. "The ISIS people chop off the heads and they then go back to their homes and they talk. And they hear we're talking about waterboarding like it's the worst thing in the world, and they've just drowned 100 people and chopped off 50 heads. They must think we are a little bit on the weak side. . . . We are playing by rules, but they have no rules. It's very hard to win when that's the case," he argued.[34]

While there sometimes can be cycles of virtuosity in which good deeds in one place inspire similar deeds elsewhere, it also is the case that bad deeds can cause vitriol elsewhere. Extremism and violence are especially prone to generating overreaction because they poison the well for societal or international cooperation. It is surprisingly easy to spread "misinformation" or "unverified rumors" through online media, especially when people's information sources are narrow in nature and the social system is polarized.[35]

American Enterprise Institute President Arthur Brooks has written about "'motive attribution asymmetry,' in which proponents of each side of an argument attributed their own group's aggressive behavior to love, but the opposite side's to hatred." He argues that "millions of Americans believe that their side is basically benevolent while the other side is evil and out to get them."[36] This kind of attribution inevitably hardens views about both domestic and foreign adversaries.

In this situation, it is easy for political leaders to point to excesses in other places to justify their own extreme steps. They denounce real or imagined adversaries and use their own strong response to solidify political support. Extremist attacks also can be used to explain the need to spend more on defense, engage in surveillance of enemies, or even go to war. What Brooks calls the "victimhood culture" makes it difficult for people to understand the viewpoints of others or see that foes might have reasonable or valid positions. Empathy and tolerance are in short supply in a world filled with extremism and zealotry.

In today's world, there are few penalties for taking extreme political positions. Some people glorify radical ideas as "out-of-the-box" or bold and visionary. Playing to the base has become a common tactic. Political leaders use strategies that target the angriest and most vocal among their own supporters; this is one way of being assured of core support. In the words of political scientists Jacob Hacker and Paul Pierson, the "race to the base" has become the dominant political strategy in many countries.[37]

Some argue that political polarization makes it difficult to adopt large-scale remedies due to the tendency of democratic institutions to be gridlocked. But the experience of recent decades shows that legislative inaction also creates frustration and encourages leaders to think of new solutions. Ironically, political paralysis can lead to far-reaching ideas that are revolutionary in nature. High levels of polarization can push the public's appetite for change, sometimes even just for the sake of change. Radical ideas that previously would have been discredited now garner serious debate. This was confirmed by a Quinnipiac University survey in 2016 that found two-thirds of U.S. voters agreed with the statement that "the old way of doing things no longer works and we need radical change."[38]

Polarization speeds up change in another way, too. Political parties fight to control the government, and when they attain power they realize they have limited time to get things done. In a gridlocked epoch, people are impatient for action. As explained by Republican Senator Cory Gardner of Colorado, "The temperament of the electorate is getting shorter. The American public is no longer giving people time to turn the ship around. They're wanting it done in two years. So in two years if we don't perform, the same kind of wave election is coming back in 2016 except in the opposite direction."[39]

Impatience leads politicians to confront adversaries, advocate massive reforms, and—for the short period when they hold a political advantage—attempt far-reaching policies that they think will transform the country.[40] Rather than generating no change or small-scale alterations, gridlock and polarization encourage attempts at large-scale policymaking. Leaders often have just a few months or a year where they are in control of government and therefore in a position to act. If they don't take action, someone else is likely to do so and gain an advantage over them. As noted in a speech by singer Bob Dylan, "Times always change. They really do. And you have to always be ready for something that's coming along and you never expected it."[41]

Plan of the Book

My approach in this book is to use a series of case studies to illustrate the scope and nature of megachange. I include examples from global affairs, American politics, and political developments in other countries to demonstrate how large-scale change happens and how it affects politics and policy. The world is deeply interconnected in an age of globalization and what happens locally can reverberate in many other places.

Chapter 2 looks at examples of megachange in foreign affairs such as globalization, 9/11 terrorism, the Arab Spring uprising, Russia's Crimea invasion, the 2015 *Charlie Hebdo* murders and Paris attacks, and the Brexit referendum in the United Kingdom. An era that started with an emphasis on international cooperation and trade agreements thought to benefit many different nations has ended in a period of global strife, intense conflict, and disputes over religion, economics, and politics. The hope of globalization has given rise to the fear and anxiety of international terrorism and military aggression, and discontent regarding whether globalization represents a desirable course of action.

Chapter 3 presents case studies of several domestic policies and trends that have undergone large shifts. It investigates religious revival, the Reagan Revolution, Obamacare, same-sex marriage, marijuana legalization, income inequality, Trumpism, and border protection. Across a period of several decades, the United States moved from a time of political conservatism to a complex blend of social liberalism and nationalistic sentiments. There have been profound shifts in public opinion and public policy in a number of areas. Terrorism has pushed many Americans toward tougher reactions, and the subsequent U.S. policy choices have inflamed opinions abroad.

Chapter 4 discusses examples of Thermidorian reactions in megachange. During a period of transformation, moves and countermoves often show major fluctuations from side to side. I look at how liberal protests in the 1960s spawned conservative reactions, alterations in attitudes about smoking, shifts in public sentiments about the HIV/AIDS virus, the Catholic Church transition from Popes John Paul II and Benedict XVI to Pope Francis, and changing views about diplomatic relations with Cuba. Large shifts in one direction mobilize countershifts from opponents upset with the transformation. The result often is incomplete revolutions.

Chapter 5 investigates the complications of religious zealotry in large-scale change. Religious intensity is one of the factors that have fueled megachange at home and abroad. I look at how fundamentalism in Judaism, Islam, and Christianity affects global affairs and domestic politics. There are clashes of values both across and within each of these great faiths. Disagreements in these areas have had dramatic impact on many contemporary issues, encouraged extreme behavior, and discouraged the tolerance and mutual understanding that people need in an interconnected world.

Chapter 6 argues that during a period of megachange we need to find ways to deal with individual, societal, and governance challenges. Adjusting to a faster and larger-scale nature of change requires basic adjustments in institutional arrangements and governance strategies. Many of our traditional political processes are geared toward slow deliberation and incremental change. With extremism on the rise and comprehensive policymaking in vogue, we need to alter our institutions to cope with fast-changing developments.

Chapter 7 explores strategies for dealing with megachange. People need to broaden their horizons, find anchors that help them deal with large-scale transformations, understand that small shifts can have tremendous impacts over time, and end the winner-take-all mentality that elevates the stakes of great change. Unless we learn how to deradicalize civil society, it will be difficult to solve contemporary problems.

Chapter 8 concludes the book by looking at several political, economic, and existential possibilities for future megachange. They include Iran (or non-state terrorists) getting a nuclear bomb, robots taking a high proportion of jobs, global warming flooding the coasts, Europe turning right and undermining democracy, and microbial life found to be existing around the universe. Each of these scenarios represents plausible possibilities for large-scale transformation. We need to anticipate their emergence and determine how to deal with them before they provoke full-blown crises.

CHAPTER 2

Shocks in Foreign Affairs

Continuity is simpler to analyze than change. The projection of existing patterns into the future is straightforward and clear cut. Little insight is required other than determining what the situation is today and extrapolating accordingly, while taking into account the possibility of minor adjustments.

Yet status quo models don't explain the tremendous shifts that have taken place internationally in recent years. There have been tectonic shifts on many fronts from superpower relations and global commerce to the rise of terrorism and virulence of nonstate actors. The emergence of ungoverned spaces has destabilized the international order and generated considerable chaos and disorder.

In looking at models of change, it is apparent there are many causes of global transformation. Factors such as economic disruptions, military conflict, religious strife, and governance failures have produced dramatic alterations in foreign affairs. Developments in one area can reverberate elsewhere.[1] This insight was noted long ago by weather expert Edward Lorenz, when he asked whether "the flapping of a butterfly's wings in

Brazil set off a tornado in Texas."[2] Through his assessment of multiplier rates, interactions, and compound effects, he noted that small-scale events can have far-reaching ramifications on the global landscape.[3]

In this chapter, I review several examples of major alterations in foreign affairs, including the impact of globalization, the Arab Spring, Russia's invasion and annexation of Crimea, terrorist attacks in the United States and Europe, and the United Kingdom referendum, popularly referred to as Brexit, which allowed British voters to say whether they wanted the UK to leave the European Union (EU). These cases describe events that developed quickly and had widespread domestic and international consequences. Over a period of a few decades, the world has gone from hope that globalization and increased trade would lead to greater international peace and prosperity to an environment that is marked by fear, chaos, and disorder.

Globalization

The fall of the Berlin Wall and the subsequent end of communist governments in Russia, Eastern Europe, and Central Asia seemed to harken a new world. The old period of bipolar conflict between the United States and Soviet Union gave rise, briefly in the 1990s, to an era dominated by the West, especially the United States. Widespread hope arose that a new order would be based not on conflict but on free trade, liberalized investment rules, international commerce, and improved global understanding.[4]

Undergirding all of these transformations was a worldview that encouraged countries to work together to advance economically, politically, and culturally. The idea was that governments could negotiate agreements that would improve trade, standardize capital and investment requirements, decrease global conflict, and lead to better international relations.

Francis Fukuyama was among those celebrating this new era, boldly proclaiming the "end of history"—meaning a dramatic decrease in international conflict associated with competing ideologies.[5] Rather than a world wracked by intense disputes between capitalism and communism, this interpretation forecast the rise of a universal order that could reconcile disparate economic and political interests.

In the same era, countries negotiated major agreements designed to improve international trade and commerce. One of the most important came in regard to trade, when the United States ratified the North American Free Trade Agreement (NAFTA) in 1993, which promised increased commerce with Canada and Mexico. That agreement repealed major tariffs and trade restrictions among the three countries, making it easier for businesses to ship products and services across national boundaries.

This regional trade initiative—the first of many around the world—was followed by the entry of China into the World Trade Organization in 2001. China agreed to open up its economy and expand trade and commerce with other countries. Some limited foreign investment in China was allowed, internal markets were opened to some extent, and tariffs were reduced. The result was a dramatic expansion in China's global trade. Within a few years, that country became the world's greatest manufacturing center and was exporting goods around the globe and thus building its economic power.

Two international agreements that took effect in 1995, establishing the World Trade Organization and creating the General Agreement on Trade in Services (GATS), also sought to reduce tariffs across many nations and remove protectionist features. Countries with large public ownership of business assets were encouraged to privatize them and adopt policies that expanded the private sector.

Internationally, the United States led multilateral efforts to forge common foreign policies. For example, in 1995 after Bosnian Serbs killed some 7,000 Muslims in the town of Sarajevo at the height of a civil war, a NATO alliance assembled by America bombed Belgrade and forced it to negotiate a peace treaty that ended the war and established a multiethnic political system for Bosnia and Herzegovina.

Since the late 1990s, the European Union has dropped border controls and most EU member nations have adopted the euro as their joint currency. This facilitated travel and trade across the continent and encouraged cross-border flows. Countries that previously had been military and economic competitors pledged to cooperate with one another and adopt joint policies on economic development, government regulation, and foreign policy. The downside of these steps became clear only after the 2008 global financial crisis, when the EU was forced to bail out Greece and several other countries facing possible bankruptcy.

Not everyone was persuaded that globalization was beneficial. Some critics complained that free trade was unjust and benefited developed nations over those of the developing world. Others argued the opposite—that increased trade came at the expense of manufacturing jobs in the United States and other developed countries because multinational corporations engaged in a "race to the bottom" in search of the lowest possible wages for workers. There were street protests around major trade meetings and charges that Western multinational corporations and investors had unfair advantages in trade and commerce that would exacerbate global inequality.

Yet despite these dissonant notes, for a while world leaders argued that the peace and prosperity unleashed by globalization would tame international disputes and usher in a bright future for most people. It was hoped that countries that previously had been adversaries (such as China and the United States) would find common ground and reach agreements that were helpful to each side. Some progress was made during the 1990s on other global issues, including limited agreements to tackle the increasingly ominous threat of climate change. However, the good feelings generated by globalization eventually gave way to discord, especially after international terrorists engineered a stunning attack on the epicenter of the Western establishment.

9/11 Terrorism

The new global order was shocked on September 11, 2001, when a plane crashed into one of the New York City World Trade Center towers at 8:46 a.m. At first, observers wondered if this were some type of freak accident. But when another plane hit the second tower at 9:03 a.m., a third plane crashed into the Pentagon in Washington at 9:37 a.m., and a fourth plane crash-landed in a Pennsylvania field, it became obvious that someone, or some group, had launched a systematic assault on leading symbols of American economic and political power. It was clear that these attacks would have serious ramifications on public opinion and public policy.[6]

Within two hours, both Trade Center towers had collapsed, nearly 3,000 people were killed, and another 6,000 injured. The stunning use by nineteen hijackers of jetliners packed with ordinary people to attack major buildings was absolutely shocking—not just for the horror it represented, but as a vivid indication that the world had irrevocably changed. The idea that terrorists from outside a country could attack the United States and inflict huge fatalities on unarmed people deeply frightened the entire nation.

No longer would the United States or Western Europe be isolated from international terrorism that already had become common in the Middle East and parts of Asia, Latin America, and Africa. The 9/11 attacks would move the West back toward a more militaristic stance, similar to the early days of the Cold War. America would launch two wars (in Afghanistan and Iraq), embrace much more assertive policies on domestic surveillance and counterterrorism, and set up a prison at Guantanamo Bay on the coast of Cuba to incarcerate foreigners suspected of plotting to harm the United States.[7]

The attacks furthermore would harden American public opinion. When asked how worried they were about becoming a victim of terrorism, the proportion went from 24 percent in 2000 before the 9/11 attacks to 59 percent in 2001 after the attacks (see figure 2-1). This number stayed above 40 percent for many of the following fifteen years.[8]

A Gallup survey conducted ten years after the attacks found that 58 percent of respondents believed Americans had permanently changed the way they lived because of what had happened. When asked how their behavior had changed, 38 percent said they were less willing to travel abroad, 27 percent indicated they were less likely to attend large events, 24 percent were less willing to fly on airplanes, and 20 percent were less likely to go into skyscrapers.[9]

There were equally dramatic increases in public concern about terrorism in Europe, Asia, and Africa. President George W. Bush was perhaps the chief political beneficiary of the changed public opinion. His job approval rating jumped from 51 percent in September 2001, right before the attacks, to 90 percent later in the month, based on his tough response. This support would remain above 80 percent through March 2002, half a year after the attacks, and would contribute to his electoral success in 2004.[10]

The high level of political support, along with the reluctance

FIGURE 2-1. *Public Worry about Terrorism in the United States, 2000–15*

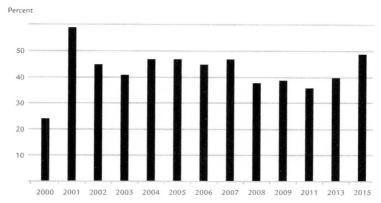

Source: Gallup Poll, "Terrorism in the United States," June 2–7, 2015.

of many Democrats to be critical during a time of national unity, enabled Bush to enact numerous policy changes that otherwise would have been extremely controversial. In short order, Congress approved the USA PATRIOT Act that allowed search warrants of U.S. homes and businesses without prior notification. It required financial institutions and telecommunications companies secretly to give the government information about financial transactions and online behavior. And it enabled intelligence agencies to acquire "metadata" revealing the times and dates of phone numbers that people called, plus the duration of the conversations.[11]

Privacy and civil liberty advocates eventually pushed back against government surveillance. They argued that these measures were overly intrusive and not effective at stopping terrorist attacks. They sought to move the country toward a posture that was protective of civil liberties. Eventually, as the immediate impacts of the 9/11 attacks faded, support grew for rolling back some of the antiterrorism responses. Congress voted in 2015 to stop the bulk collection of phone metadata and passed laws limiting certain types of surveillance.

However, after a young Muslim couple shot and killed fourteen people in San Bernardino, California, late in 2015, American political leaders such as Donald Trump pushed for tougher measures against terrorism. The country swung back to supporting vigorous measures to protect personal security, and calls for renewed surveillance reverberated around the land.

Similar to the reaction after 9/11, these moves aroused concern abroad. Many Muslims feared that America was launching a war on Islam. An expansion of government surveillance and the increasing use of unmanned drones to attack terrorism targets in Afghanistan, Iraq, Pakistan, and Somalia reinforced doubts abroad about American foreign policy. The anger unleashed by the repeated killing by the United States of innocent civilians, along with suspected terrorists, would upset global affairs, disrupt ruling regimes, and lead to counterattacks against U.S. and European targets.

The Arab Spring Uprising

For centuries, many countries in the Middle East and North Africa were run by colonial rulers, feudal families, sheiks, or emirs. Starting in the middle of the twentieth century, some of the region's authoritarian regimes were financed by money from oil sales, making it seem impossible to unseat them.

Yet brewing beneath their autocratic rule was substantial public dissatisfaction. A major divide between the small number of haves and the vast majority of have-nots existed in many of these nations. And they also suffered from high youth unemployment rates. Women had few opportunities for education or basic rights. Those who adhered to traditional religious beliefs were unhappy with the secular style of many of these regimes, while Saudi Arabia, by far the richest country in the region, was ruled by a single, extended family that had imposed a starkly fundamentalist form of Islam. Deeply embedded government corruption throughout the region meant that only the politically connected could succeed.

Courageous individuals spoke out against their rulers, only to find themselves in prison, forced into exile, or killed. Then in December 2010 a street vendor in Tunisia named Mohamed Bouazizi set himself on fire to protest confiscation of his fruit stock. His death two weeks later attracted tremendous attention and went viral throughout the region.[12]

Antigovernment activists took advantage of digital platforms such as Twitter and Facebook to spread the word about his plight and that of other dissidents. With new communications tools, outrage can expand exponentially around any region and even the world.[13] Autocracy was wrong and needed to be fought, critics argued.

Massive demonstrations, collectively known as the Arab Spring, erupted in several countries across the region.[14] Public rebellions toppled entrenched rulers in Tunisia, Egypt, and Libya, and led to civil war in Syria and Yemen. What would have been unimaginable a few years earlier saw the imprisonment and 2011 trial of Egyptian President Hosni Mubarak (although he later was released) and the killing of Libyan leader Muammar Qaddafi that same year.

Within a short time, though, the grassroots revolutions took unexpected detours. Arab Spring protests had toppled authoritarian regimes but, except in Tunisia, ultimately led to chaos or new forms of dictatorial military rule, notably in Egypt, the most populous Arab country. In the period right after Mubarak was removed from office, Egypt held a democratic election in 2012 with multiple candidates and parties vying for public support. Mohamed Morsi of the Freedom and

Independent Justice Party won the presidency with 51.7 percent of the vote. He was the nominee of the Muslim Brotherhood and became the first democratically elected head of state in that country.[15]

But Morsi's presidency did not last long. In the following year, he was ousted by the military and sentenced after a show trial to twenty years in prison for torturing protesters. His Islamist party was outlawed and its other leaders arrested. Nearly all of them ended up in jail, and some eventually were given the death sentence.[16] An army general, Abdel el-Sisi, became president and members of the armed forces regained control over the government.

In Libya, Qaddafi's demise—partly as the result of U.S. military intervention—led to complete chaos and a failed state with large amounts of ungoverned spaces. An American diplomatic post in Benghazi was burned and the ambassador died of smoke inhalation. Dueling warlords seized control of different areas and competed for control of financial and political power. Libya's destabilization had huge consequences for the entire area.[17] It contributed to a wave of large migrations to Europe and even stimulated other conflicts when Qaddafi's vast weapons arsenals leaked into neighboring countries.

The prolonged civil war in Syria has had especially tragic consequences, both within the region and even in Europe. The unresolved conflict between forces loyal to and opposed to President Bashar al-Assad has now dragged on for more than five years, killed more than 250,000 people as of early 2016 according to the United Nations, and forced more than half the population to flee their homes—including some 4.8 million who left the country altogether. The plight of Syrian exiles attempting to reach Europe caught the world's attention for much of 2015 and even led to increased support within Europe for far-right, anti-immigrant political parties. The power vacuum in much of Syria, along with continuing instability in neighboring Iraq, allowed the Islamic State of Iraq and Syria (ISIS), a successor to al Qaeda, to gain control of large sections of both countries.

The dramatic turn of events following the Arab Spring led many to wonder why the grassroots rebellions failed and generated authoritarian counter-responses and conflict. Writer Ivan Krastev argues that the conservative and militaristic backlash resulted from societal polarization and a subsequent public desire for social and political stability.[18] That sentiment allowed a new generation of strong men to emerge in several countries and dominate local politics.[19] Rather than a flowering of peace and democracy, the Arab Spring led to renewed authoritarianism and military rule in some places, with chaos, disorder, and civil war elsewhere.

Russia's Crimea Invasion

Sudden and surprising change was not limited to the Middle East. Western leaders were stunned in 2014 when Russia invaded and annexed Crimea. The peninsula had been ceded to Ukraine in 1954 by the Soviets, and no one anticipated that Russian President Vladimir Putin would brazenly violate Ukraine's national sovereignty.

Initially, the Russian president denied that his military forces were involved in the field operations. The troops had ripped off their Russian insignias to conceal their origins, but no one was fooled. Western surveillance images showed the movement of Russian troops into Crimea and eventually the eastern part of Ukraine itself. American military officials in 2015 estimated that "12,000 Russian troops are operating inside the neighboring country."[20]

At home, Russia organized national military drills involving 45,000 troops. The U.S. Navy's Northern Fleet was put on full alert in 2014, and President Putin promised to spend $340 billion over the next decade improving military capacity and fighting ability. Ominously, in 2014 there were more than 100 examples of Russian military planes flying unannounced into western European airspaces. This was triple the 2013 figure.[21]

Western leaders found themselves unable to change the new status quo. They denounced Putin's actions in many international forums and placed economic sanctions on Russia and some of its top leaders (but not Putin himself). These generally symbolic actions did not change the political reality on the ground, however. European nations had different economic interests when dealing with Russia—with many of them heavily reliant on Russian natural gas supplies—and this complicated their ability to maintain a united front.

Putin appeared to perceive Western leaders as weak and distracted, and he was able to take advantage of the fact that Western democracy can be slow and deliberate in comparison to authoritarian regimes. As was demonstrated during the European Union's handling of the euro crisis, leaders there often have difficulty reaching a consensus and making decisions. Putin had good reason to believe the West would not take meaningful action to stop his attempt to reestablish a Russian empire. He correctly gauged that neither the United States nor Europe would send in troops, or take any other meaningful action, to confront his brazen aggression.

In the end, taking control of Crimea was worth the international risks for Putin. Beyond the valuable deep seaport that was vital to the Russian navy, there were billions of gallons of oil beneath the Black Sea floor.[22] Seizing the territory of Crimea expanded Russian claims to natural assets over much of the sea. These oil reserves represented a huge bonanza for the Russian autocrat and, over the long haul, more than compensated for the short-term economic and political costs imposed by Western sanctions.

Although the seizure of Crimea weakened Putin's standing abroad, it strengthened his hand at home. Public opinion surveys initially showed him with an 86 percent approval rating within Russia, although his support fell to 61 percent in 2016 amidst low oil prices.[23] Encouraged by a fawning, state-controlled news media, many ordinary Russians cheered his nationalist moves and favored his efforts to extend the country's power. Even with a weak economy, declining oil revenues, and a devalued currency, his internal political support remained strong.

Charlie Hebdo Murders and Paris Attacks

Two brothers, Said and Cherif Kouachi, gained global attention in January 2015 when they attacked a French satirical magazine, *Charlie Hebdo,* known in large part for its caricatures of Islam. In a deadly ambush, these men entered the magazine's offices in Paris and murdered a dozen writers, editors, and other staff members.[24] It took a few days for police to find the assailants, but the shocking episode had a profound impact on the world's psyche.

The murders demonstrated what terrorist leaders long had advocated and Westerners had feared: Extremists living in the West, either acting on their own or under orders from terrorist organizations, could attack civilians to extract revenge for what they considered Western insults to the Islamic world. From their standpoint, these episodes showed the world that their sympathizers could fight back and inflict casualties on "infidels."

These attacks provoked an immediate and strong response in France and throughout the West. Almost right away, a *Je Suis Charlie* meme went viral. People endorsed the phrase as a way of demonstrating solidarity with those killed as well as signaling their opposition to terrorism; for many, the phrase also demonstrated an abhorrence of radical Islam.

The French government also moved into action. By overwhelming margins, legislators passed an intelligence-gathering bill that authorized broad surveillance powers. Government officials could tap phones and monitor home Internet behavior for evidence of terrorist activities. They also secretly could install cameras and recording devices in businesses and private residences as a way to gather information.[25]

After an abortive 2015 terrorist attack on a high-speed train from Amsterdam to Paris, leaders debated whether stricter measures were needed to ensure passenger safety. Some suggested that trains needed armed guards who would patrol the rail cars. Others proposed metal detectors to prevent riders from smuggling weapons aboard the trains.[26]

Similar to other countries that have gone through major attacks, France saw substantial shifts in domestic politics. Far-right groups, which had campaigned on the edges of the political mainstream, gained new converts. The National Front party long had warned against immigrants who undermined French culture and identity. In the wake of the *Charlie Hebdo* murders, the party quickly rose in the polls and used its new-found prominence to rail against Islamic terrorists. One of its party leaders, David Rachline, warned, "Surely we can no longer wonder whether there might be some connection between this lightning-fast rise of radical fundamentalist Islam and this rampant immigration. . . . In Europe recently, all the terrorists are Muslims."[27]

The same was true elsewhere in Europe. Alexander Gauland, a leader in the Alternative for Germany, an anti-immigrant party, argued that Islam threatened German culture. Speaking after the Hebdo attack, he said, "This bloodshed shows that anyone who ignored or laughed off the concerns about the threat Islamism poses is a fool."[28]

His sharp rhetoric was consistent with the results of a 2014 national survey in Germany. When asked whether Islam is "incompatible with the Western world," 61 percent of non-Muslim Germans answered yes.[29] That sentiment showed how significant the cultural and religious shifts had become in many European countries.

Public attitudes against terrorism hardened further following the November 2015 attacks in Paris, March 2016 bombings in Brussels, and a July 2016 truck attack in Nice. In the former, 130 people were killed in six coordinated attacks on a concert hall, restaurants, and sports stadium. French President Francois Hollande described the onslaught as "an act of war that was committed by a terrorist army, a jihadist army, Daesh [one name for ISIS], against France."[30] In the Brussels attack, thirty-one were killed and more than 230 were injured. Terrorism expert Rik Coolsaet noted that "this is a kind of scenario every capital in Europe feared since the November attacks last year. A mixture of foreign fighters coming back with experience, local sympathizers on the other hand. You have such a large number of soft targets, and you cannot secure all of them."[31]

As with the 9/11 attacks in the United States, people around the globe were shocked at the brazenness of the violence and the ability of a small group of assailants to inflict so much terror in Western societies. "They did not give anybody a chance," bemoaned one French witness.[32] In Paris, the terrorists used automatic weapons to kill large numbers of innocent people who were having dinner and enjoying Western music. In Brussels, the assailants used suicide bombs laced with nails to inflict maximum damage on a crowded air terminal and metro stop.

Worried about a repeat of the violence, France and Belgium each declared a national emergency and rounded up hundreds of suspected terrorists. Using emergency powers, the police detained people without warrants, put suspects under house arrest, banned large gatherings, and engaged in stop-and-search missions.[33] France adopted these broad powers for three months as it grappled with the aftermath of the attacks.

The French military also attacked ISIS targets in Raqqa, Syria. France bombed sites in the self-proclaimed capital of the ISIS "caliphate" in an effort to disrupt its leadership and weaken its ability to engage in other attacks. With French men and women eager to join the counter-response, military enlistments quintupled in the weeks following the attacks.[34]

In the United Kingdom, which had suffered its own terrorist attacks with bombings of transport systems in 2005, public concern developed after a 2016 survey of British Muslims showed negative attitudes toward homosexuality and women's rights. The poll, for example, revealed that 52 percent of Muslims believed that homosexuality should be illegal. In addition, 39 percent told interviewers that "wives should always obey their husbands," and one-quarter of respondents "favored replacing the British legal system with Islamic law."[35] Even though there was no comparative sample of non-Muslims, it is safe to say that these numbers likely were far higher than would be the case among more secular elements within British society.

Islamist-inspired terrorism and longstanding cultural divisions between some Muslims and non-Muslims raised new questions about national security and the integration of Muslims into European societies. These questions became even more urgent and politically sensitive throughout 2016 when more than one million refugees from Syria, North Africa, and Afghanistan tried to reach Europe and its open borders. The plight of the refugees, many of whom drowned when trying to cross the Mediterranean Sea in rickety boats, captured international attention but also put enormous pressure on European leaders. The response varied from German Chancellor Angela Merkel's willingness to accept hundreds of thousands of refugees to more hardline stances in Austria, Hungary, and other countries where citizens and leaders felt overwhelmed by the numbers of refugees. The tensions unleashed by the flood of refugees would unsettle the politics in most of Europe.

Brexit

An enormous—and in many ways surprising—megachange shock occurred on June 23, 2016, when British voters approved a public referendum to leave the European Union (EU), which had been established in 1993 through the Maastricht Treaty as an outgrowth of earlier collaborations such as the European Economic Community. The idea behind the EU was to move European nation-states to a single market by integrating customs, passport control, currencies, and overall economic development. Alongside the security agreements established through the North American Treaty Organization, the hope was that European integration would reduce the ultra-nationalism that had plagued the continent for centuries.

Initially, integration appeared to go well. Seeking to ameliorate fears and anxieties, the EU used a series of incremental steps to phase in various measures. For example, passport controls were eliminated between member countries of the EU's "Schengen Area" in 1995, and currencies were integrated in 2002 in the form of the euro. By 2020 European nations planned to move toward a digital single market that would integrate Internet policy.[36]

However, so-called euroskeptics at various stages of the process expressed doubts about the value of these policy shifts. They worried that national identity was being lost and that some countries were becoming less prosperous. The loss of manufacturing jobs in certain places, combined with stagnating incomes and rising debt levels, intensified public discontent regarding the value of integration.

One sign of serious problems came in a financial crisis involving Greek debt. Over a period of time, that Mediterranean country had accumulated a sovereign debt totaling 323 billion euros.[37] Facing the aftermath of the Great Recession, it defaulted on parts of this debt in 2012 and was not able to make a 2015 loan repayment to the International Monetary Fund. For a while, it looked like Greece might collapse and take other Southern European economies down with it. At the last minute, though, the crisis was averted when Greece agreed to a series of fiscal steps designed to shore up its budget and avoid further defaults.

But new trouble ensued when civil war and unrest in North Africa and the Middle East led to a wave of refugees seeking sanctuary in Europe. According to data from the EU statistics agency, 1.26 million people sought asylum in Europe in 2015.[38] Facing violence in Syria, Libya, Iraq, and Afghanistan, among other places, they sought a better future in spots such as Germany, Hungary, Sweden, and France. About one-third of these individuals came from Syria, while others migrated from Afghanistan, Kosovo, Albania, Pakistan, Eritrea, and Nigeria.

The large number of migrants increased fears among native-born Europeans about national sovereignty, economic prospects, cultural integration, and personal security. Many of the new immigrants were Muslim and therefore came from different religious and cultural backgrounds. Would they integrate into Western societies and accept basic values such as religious tolerance and cultural pluralism? Would there be an increase in terrorist attacks? Many were not convinced that integration was the right course of action.

First in Hungary and Poland and then in the Netherlands, Norway, and elsewhere, nationalist forces warned about the dangers of large-scale immigration resulting from Europe's open borders. They claimed the new entrants could not be trusted and argued they would draw on government benefits without adding much to the economy or society at large. Rather than accept longstanding values embracing cultural tolerance, a growing number of political leaders argued it was time to build walls and restrict access to their countries in order to keep out those who they feared might take away jobs, as well as immigrants they called terrorists, vagrants, and ne'er-do-wells. From this nationalist vantage point, the economic, political, and cultural risks of open borders and immigration simply outweighed any possible benefits.

These concerns came to a head in the United Kingdom as that nation debated its relationship to the EU. Hoping to quell long-term dissension within his own Conservative party about European integration, Prime Minister David Cameron called for a public referendum to resolve the issue. He argued that the benefits of remaining within the EU were substantial, but other party leaders such as former London Mayor Boris Johnson disputed those claims. Johnson—who previously had supported Britain's EU membership—early in 2016 suddenly joined with EU opponents in arguing that the UK needed to exercise tighter control over border security, that immigration was growing too fast, and that the country could do better economically on its own. The whole point of sovereignty, they argued, was to control the country's own destiny.

When citizens went to the polls, they voted 52 to 48 percent to leave the European Union.[39] The stunning reversal of national policy caused a massive fall of the British pound, upset financial markets around the world, and shocked leaders who had hoped and believed the referendum would reaffirm the status quo. The vote also renewed the prospect that Scotland might secede from the United Kingdom, since a strong majority of Scottish voters supported staying in the EU. Although opinion polls had predicted a close vote, few in the business and political elite really anticipated this disruption and therefore were shocked when a significant majority of voters cast their ballots against the EU.

According to Article 50 of the Lisbon Treaty, Britain and the EU could take up to two years to negotiate the terms of withdrawal. There remain many complicated questions concerning whether the referendum could be ignored or reversed, whether

Britain could somehow negotiate a new status outside the EU but still enjoy some of the benefits of membership, and what Britain's withdrawal would mean in the long term for the EU itself. At the very least, there will be many months—and probably years—of uncertainty as leaders seek to navigate the future path.

While the British debated the electoral aftermath, nationalist political leaders in other European nations pushed for EU referenda in their own countries. For example, French National Front leader Marine Le Pen praised the UK move and said, "Across Europe, I hope that initiatives will emerge to cause as many replicas as possible of this Brexit. Movement has been triggered toward the end of the European Union as we know it."[40] Similar comments came from nationalist politicians in Denmark, the Netherlands, Finland, and Austria. Amid all the debate, no one was sure whether the UK vote was the first domino signaling the disintegration of Europe.

Dramatic Consequences

Big, surprising events have taken place throughout world history. There have been lengthy wars, economic disruptions, and political revolutions on a grand scale. Those events have marked a number of periods from the Renaissance and Reformation to the Industrial Revolution and beyond. Megashifts have altered governments, societies, and international relationships in many historical eras and transformed how people live and relate to one another.

But contemporary global affairs appear to be unusually chaotic and volatile in nature. Power alignments have shifted, failed states have proliferated, nonstate actors have sparked violence in many countries, and terrorism has increased public anxiety and generated demands for tough action. Regional groupings such as the European Union that were thought to be quite stable now are under duress and may even split apart.

There are reasons why we have entered a period of mega-change. Many of the forces that used to constrain change have grown weak. Radicalization and extremism have proliferated and altered a wide range of international relationships. The bipolar world has shifted to a multipolar dynamic with the emergence of new powers. Conventional international norms have frayed and there are significant challenges to established economic regimes based on globalization and the free flow of people, goods, and services across boundaries.

As pointed out in this chapter, globalization several decades ago encouraged leaders and workers to believe that increased trade and commerce would bring peace and broadened prosperity worldwide. The view was that this new paradigm would benefit nearly everyone and promote improved economic and political integration. These perceptions guided many of the trade agreements and international treaties that were negotiated during this period.

Yet subsequent terrorism, wars, and protectionist sentiments have proved that globalization is not sacrosanct. The negative aspects of that doctrine—notably the shift of manufacturing jobs from Western industrialized countries to China and other places where labor was cheap—led many in the West to wonder what was gained from free and open trade. The 9/11 attacks in the United States and similar ones in Europe, as well as blatant Russian aggression, galvanized Western policymakers and heightened fears among the general public. Both rhetoric and actions have turned tougher, and there have been calls to amend or revoke trade agreements and reallocate public resources to national security.

Things that were considered stable and secure are now up for national and international debate. Foreign attacks increased antiterrorist sentiment at home and inflamed tensions with those such as Muslims who were perceived as outsiders. In an era of instant global communications, uncompromising language quickly spreads internationally. For example, while Westerners worried about terrorist attacks and feared Muslims who were not well-integrated within their countries, Muslims worried about a Western war against Islam, including high-profile calls to bar them from the United States. Extremism abroad has encouraged extremism at home, and vice versa.

The anger and anxiety evident in many places have torpedoed the optimistic hopes of several decades ago that globalization would transform the world in an entirely positive direction. Rather than enjoying an era of universal peace and prosperity, citizens in many countries worry that their economic fortunes have been undermined by global trade agreements, and they are fearful of attacks by foreign terrorists or a deranged "lone wolf" acting at home.

In a rather short period of time, the good feelings that once surrounded globalization have given way to discordant notes and intense conflict in much of the world. The rapid way in which the international order disintegrated suggests that stability is overrated and transformation can happen quickly. Just because things seem stable and continuous at one point in time does not mean they will stay that way indefinitely. As *Washington Post* columnist E. J. Dionne pointed out, we should avoid the trap of presentism, which leads people to believe that continuity always is going to outweigh change.[41]

CHAPTER 3

Shifts in Domestic Politics

Public opinion in the United States often is thought to be relatively stable. According to political scientists Benjamin Page and Robert Shapiro in their book, *The Rational Public*, overall citizen views don't change radically over short periods of time.[1] People's opinions about public affairs are deeply rooted in party identifications and ideology, along with personal perceptions related to fundamental issues such as the economy, war, and peace. For those reasons, their perspectives evolve slowly based on social, economic, and political developments.

Yet in recent decades, there have been examples of major shifts in American public opinion, personal behavior, and public policy. Important alterations have taken place on different issues and in the fortunes of political parties. In some cases, the fluctuations have arisen from the grassroots, while in other examples, they have been driven from the top down.

In this chapter, I look at several cases of substantial opinion and policy change in the United States. Among the topics covered include a religious revival, the Reagan revolution, marijuana legalization, same-sex marriage, Obamacare, income inequality, Trumpism, and concerns about border security.

Each of these developments illustrates how large-scale shifts take place and dramatically affect domestic affairs. In a rather short period of time, U.S. policy has shifted from religious and political conservatism to social liberalism on lifestyle issues alongside nationalistic concerns about security, terrorism, and global affairs.

Religious Revival

When I was growing up in rural southwest Ohio in the 1960s, the pace of life seemed quite glacial. In the small farming community where I was raised, grandparents lived next to their adult children and anchored family life. People went to the local church and learned the same religious and political beliefs that had guided previous generations.

Signs of change came in the 1960s and 1970s, though. There were many types of political and social adjustments taking place in much of the country. This included the rise of environmentalism, the women's rights movement, the civil rights movement, states' rights in response to progressive national legislation, and a burgeoning tax revolt in some states and localities.

Some of these conflicting tenets hit my tiny hamlet in 1970 when people at our local Presbyterian Church discovered that the national presbytery, the ruling body for the U.S. denomination, had given $10,000 to the Angela Davis Legal Defense Fund. This was in keeping with the liberalism of many urban areas and the social movements then sweeping the country. Progressive efforts to fight racism, sexism, and overall conservatism would unleash a counter-revolution both from my small community and the Bible Belt in general.[2]

Davis, a young black Californian philosopher, had become a cause célèbre in the country's liberal community following her indictment for conspiracy to commit homicide and kidnapping. She was a "black power" activist who worked as an organizer for the Black Panthers. A friend of hers named Jonathan Jackson had attempted to help his brother George, a member of the "Soledad Three"—men who had killed a guard at the Soledad Prison in California—break out of the Marin County Hall of Justice on August 7, 1970.[3]

During the failed shootout, several people were killed, including George Jackson, then on trial, and Judge Harold Haley. When Jonathan Jackson's gun, used to shoot Haley, was discovered to have been registered in the name of Davis, the FBI placed her on its most wanted list. At that time she was only the third woman to find herself with this designation. For two months she was at large, but eventually she was captured and placed in prison.

Around the country, social justice activists accused the government of undertaking an illegal vendetta against her. She was an avowed communist who had been fired from a teaching job at the University of California–Los Angeles by Governor Ronald Reagan the year before. She had been active in a number of causes centering on race, class, and gender inequity. Musicians John Lennon and Yoko Ono wrote a song named "Angela" that called for her acquittal on charges of abetting the courthouse shootings. For many, she was a political prisoner.[4]

Although the United Presbyterian Church had many conservative congregations around the country, the New York City headquarters took a distinctively liberal line on issues of race and gender. During its 183rd General Assembly, the church's council on church and race indicated it had given money to the Marin County Black Defense Fund to provide legal help for Angela Davis. According to social activists, "African American Presbyterians responded to Angela Davis's situation as a black woman whose right to receive a fair trial was not guaranteed in America at that time. They responded to Angela Davis as a child of God and as a black woman in racist America."[5]

When word reached my small town of Fairhaven, Ohio—with a population of a couple hundred people on a busy day—that church money had been provided for Angela Davis's legal defense, our local congregation went into an uproar over the financial support of a black communist. As an all-white community, Fairhaven wasn't big on promoting inter-racial understanding. And being a self-avowed communist was not a strong selling point in my hometown.

Conservative congregants debated what to do. Among the options were expressing outrage over the funding decision, withholding annual dues from the national Presbytery, or seceding from the national organization. The latter was a radical step because the national church owned the local church and the land on which it was based. Secession meant that the congregation would have to buy back its own church from the national organization.

After months of discussion, the elders in our congregation voted to secede from the national Presbyterian Church. The local community would buy back the sanctuary and become the Fairhaven Community Church, unaffiliated with any denomination and therefore in control of its own destiny.

It was not obvious at the time how instrumental this decision would become in later years when opposition to abortion and gay lifestyles and the teaching of evolution mobilized conservative activists around the country. But having a church freed from the strictures of the national body gave local congregations the ability to become more politically active.

Over the following decades, nondenominational, community churches would spread across the Midwest, South, and West and become powerful change agents. The number of unaffiliated local churches would grow from ten in 1970 to over 1,600 in 2011.[6] Many, especially in the growing urban areas of the South and West, would attract thousands of people each week. They would become important, sometimes dominant, forces in local society and community politics.

Freed of bureaucratic oversight, these churches would hire their own ministers and follow their own religious and political paths. Liberal church organizers on the East Coast no longer could tell local congregations what to do. Community-based churches adopted stances in keeping with local values, not liberal viewpoints common on the coasts. Religious congregations would become much more active politically and eventually would help conservative leaders win control of the American national government.

The Reagan Revolution

Republicans shocked the country in 1980 when they mobilized conservative religious and political activists and won the presidency and a majority of the seats in the Senate. Unhappy with double-digit unemployment and high inflation under Democrat Jimmy Carter, voters turned to Ronald Regan and other candidates of the right, ushering in a period of tremendous change in domestic and foreign policy.

During his first year, President Reagan—who defined big government as the nation's chief "problem" to be solved—sparked the antigovernment revolution by pushing Congress to enact across-the-board tax cuts. Operating on the assumption that the best way to alter policy in a fundamental way was to reduce revenue, the chief executive got legislators to cut taxes by 23 percent over three years and drop the top marginal rate from 70 to 50 percent. He also cut the estate tax so people could pass more of what they had accumulated to their heirs.

Having slashed taxes, Republicans worked to reduce government spending on domestic programs too. Aligning themselves with conservative Democrats upset with large government, the GOP managed to pass major budget legislation. In Reagan's first term, nondefense outlays dropped 9.7 percent, the largest reduction in the post–World War II period.[7] Areas experiencing substantial cuts included housing, urban development, transportation, and education, among others.

At the same time, Reagan increased defense spending and took a hard line toward the Soviet Union. He challenged that nation's lack of freedom and emphasis on collectivism and argued that Russian leaders needed to provide more liberty for their people. The chief executive promised Americans that he would stand up to Soviet expansionism.

To back up that stance, he raised military spending dramatically, emphasizing new generations of weapons systems, including an antimissile system that critics derided as "Star Wars." Reagan made it clear to world leaders he would intervene where he felt American interests were at stake. For example, he sent troops to the small Caribbean island of Grenada to topple what he viewed as a leftist government. The show of force sent a powerful signal to the rest of the Caribbean and Latin America that the United States was intervening in its regional sphere of influence. The United States also supported rightist guerillas fighting the leftist Sandinista regime in Nicaragua, backed a right-wing government in El Salvador against leftist guerrillas there, and stationed Marines in Lebanon in a failed effort to help end a long civil war.

In varying degrees, later GOP leaders such as President George Herbert Walker Bush, House Speaker Newt Gingrich, and President George W. Bush continued Reagan's agenda of cutting taxes and reducing the role of the federal government in key domestic areas, especially in social programs primarily benefiting the poor. Between 1972 and 2008, GOP candidates won two-thirds of the presidential elections, gained control of a majority of statehouses, and dominated political discourse across the country. Their policy views would guide public discussions and help Republicans drive the agenda of American politics for almost four decades.

Around the same time, conservative ideas about limiting the role of government would gain ascendancy in other places as well. This included conservative governments in the United Kingdom (under Margaret Thatcher), Germany (with the Helmut Kohl administration and his successors), and elsewhere. The emergence of strong conservative leaders in several Western nations would drive global and domestic affairs in a rightward direction. Social welfare programs were cut, taxes reduced, and government regulations relaxed in many areas. Liberal commentators complained about a "race to the bottom" in terms of social benefits and government programs. They feared that the conservative movement in these Western democracies were devastating the needy and exacerbating inequality.

Marijuana Legalization

In 1982 the Reagan administration launched its famous "war on drugs" that took a tough stance on a wide range of illegal narcotics. First Lady Nancy Reagan uttered the famous rallying cry that propelled this campaign. When asked by a fourth-grader in Oakland, California, what to say if a person offered her drugs, Mrs. Reagan replied: "Just say no."[8] With the ear of the president and other leaders, the first lady spearheaded state and national legislation that toughened penalties for illegal drug possession and sale.

In 1994 President Bill Clinton and the Republican Congress built on this stance by increasing criminal penalties for a variety of drug offenses. Saying that "gangs and drugs have taken over our streets," Clinton signed a bill that imposed longer sentences for federal crimes, expanded use of the death penalty, and provided billions in federal money for states and localities to hire additional law enforcement officers and construct new prisons.[9]

This new federal approach built on "three strikes and you are out" laws in California and dozens of other states. Habitual offenders, meaning those who had been convicted of at least two violent offenses, could be sentenced to prison terms of twenty-five years or more. The stated goal was to take violent criminals out of circulation and make society safer.

The result of these policy changes was a dramatic increase in mass incarceration and the rise of what became known as the "penal state."[10] In short order, the United States had the highest incarceration rate among developed nations and one of the highest rates in the world. According to research by Lauren Glaze, Erinn Herberman, and Gary Walmsley, America imprisons 710 people per 100,000 residents, which far surpasses the rates of 210 found in Mexico, 147 in the United Kingdom, 118 in Canada, 79 in Germany, and 51 in Japan. Overall, around 7 million adults are in the U.S. correctional system.[11] According to the Federal Bureau of Prisons, almost half (47 percent) of the people in federal incarceration are there on drug offenses.[12]

This high level of imprisonment imposes a number of fiscal, personal, and social costs. States and localities are struggling to finance the prisons required for all these inmates, and prison overcrowding has become a major problem in some states, notably California. At a time when there is great need for spending on education, health care, housing, and infrastructure, vital resources are going to incarceration. In many states, the correctional system has been the fastest-growing part of the budget for many years.[13]

Figure 3-1 shows state prison spending from 1982 to 2010. At the beginning of this period, states spent $15 billion annually on corrections, but that amount more than tripled to nearly $50 billion by 2010. During this same period, the number of individuals incarcerated went from 371,522 to 1,316,858. This was a 400 percent increase in state prison population.[14]

Those who get out of jail invariably struggle to find their way. In an era of instant background checks, it is very difficult for ex-convicts to find jobs. Most employment applications ask about past convictions, and checking that box disqualifies many from gainful employment. The high unemployment of ex-cons increases recidivism, complicates their financial well-being, and disrupts family life. Being an ex-con virtually guarantees economic struggles long after leaving prison.

Many former prisoners lose their right to vote and therefore are unable to participate in decisions affecting their lives. At a time when the political system makes many choices that restrict their options, ex-cons cannot participate in a key aspect of civic life and affect societal deliberations. They cannot cast ballots against politicians who pursue punitive measures against nonviolent offenders.

Equally important is the social impact of incarceration. There are dramatic differentials in imprisonment based on

FIGURE 3-1. *State Spending on Prisons, 1982–2010*

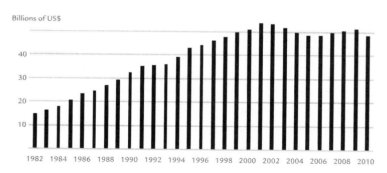

Source: Tracey Kyckelhahn, "State Corrections Expenditures, FY 1982–2010," U. S. Department of Justice Bureau of Justice Statistics, April 30, 2014.

race. According to economists Derek Neal and Armin Rick of the University of Chicago, nearly 28 percent of black men ages 20 to 34 who dropped out of high school are in prison, compared to 7 percent of white men in that age bracket with no diploma.[15]

In addition, work based on data from Bruce Western and Christopher Wildeman finds there is a "70 percent chance that an African American man without a high school diploma will be imprisoned by his mid-thirties."[16] That is a shocking number that dramatizes the dismal prospects facing those with a prison record. Many people began to feel that the previous "tough on crime" movement had gone too far and led to undesirable social, budgetary, and political consequences.

The high prison rates and convictions on drug charges of nonviolent offenders eventually stimulated a counter-movement to decriminalize and then legalize marijuana usage. One of the leading funders in this area was the late billionaire Peter Lewis. He was the chief executive officer of Progressive Insurance when his leg was amputated following a serious infection. While recuperating, he used marijuana to ease the pain and found it to have medical value. Concerned about the strict criminal penalties associated with use of the drug and having been arrested for possession in New Zealand, he spent millions supporting its legalization.[17]

As a sign of the way that wealthy individuals can drive change, he devoted more than half a million dollars to a Massachusetts ballot campaign that allowed the medicinal use of marijuana and hundreds of thousands of dollars on a similar California ballot measure. Over the past two decades, it is estimated that he spent between $40 million and $60 million on campaigns to decriminalize and legalize marijuana possession and use.[18]

Lewis was very successful in his advocacy. Colorado and Washington were early adopters of this reform. Following successful ballot campaigns, each state legalized marijuana usage and sales in 2012 and opened the first legal marketplaces in the country. This was followed by successful legalization campaigns in Alaska, Oregon, and Washington, D.C.[19]

Figure 3-2 shows the sharp changes over the last decade in the percentage of those polled who favored the legalization of marijuana. In 2004, according to Gallup surveys, only 34 percent of Americans favored legalization, but this rose to 58 percent in 2014. Conservatives were the least likely to support the idea, at 31 percent, while 73 percent of liberals and 58 percent of moderates favored it.[20]

The polls also showed substantial differences based on region and age. People in the East and West were most likely to support marijuana legalization, followed by the South (47 percent) and Midwest (45 percent). Generational variations also were apparent. Of those ages 18 to 34, 64 percent supported legalization, compared to only 41 percent of those 55 years or older.[21]

Despite these regional and generational differences, the

FIGURE 3-2. *Marijuana Legalization, 2004–14*

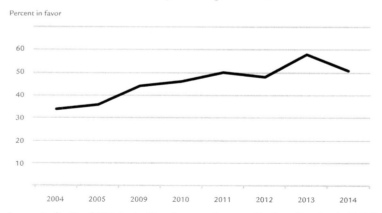

Source: Lydia Saad, "Majority Continues to Support Pot Legalization in U.S.," Gallup Poll, November 6, 2014.

overall trend seemed clear. A growing number of people no longer consider personal marijuana possession as a serious crime or even a crime at all. In dramatic fashion, they have moved substantially in the direction of supporting legalization and keeping minor offenders out of prison.

Brookings Institution scholars Philip Wallach and John Hudak have analyzed how the politics have changed. Based on public referenda, they note that "over 148 million Americans now live in pro-medical marijuana states."[22] Far from being nonmainstream, marijuana decriminalization and legalization are at the forefront of major policy change.

The economic impact has been considerable, as well. A 2015 report on marijuana by the Colorado Department of Revenue found that 833 retail licenses and 1,416 medical licenses had been established within the state and that 109,578 pounds of medical marijuana and 38,660 pounds of retail flower had been sold.[23] In addition, nearly 2 million units of medical edible products containing marijuana and 2.8 million units of retail edible products were purchased. Sales tax revenue from marijuana sales totaled $40.9 million between January and October 2014 and is growing rapidly.[24] Within a year of passage, marijuana has become a substantial business in Colorado, and other states are considering emulating its policy action.

Same-Sex Marriage

In 1996 Congress passed and President Bill Clinton signed into law the Defense of Marriage Act. This bill stipulated that recognized marriage was between a man and a woman and that states were not bound by same-sex marriage laws passed in other states. The legislation also made it clear that same-sex spouses were ineligible for federal benefits available to heterosexual couples.[25]

This law was firmly in the mainstream of public opinion at the time. Republicans held majorities in both the House and Senate and led efforts to enact the bill. Following controversies over Clinton's "don't ask, don't tell" policy for gays serving in the military and pressure from conservative activists, the legislation passed both chambers by large majorities. Clinton signed the bill in private and did not allow any cameras to record his approval—a few weeks before the presidential elections.

At the time, as shown in figure 3-3, the public generally disapproved of same-sex marriage. Indeed, Gallup survey data in 1996 revealed that only 27 percent of the American public favored same-sex marriage.[26] Many people, especially in Southern and Midwestern states, were not keen on gay rights in general or same-sex marriage in particular. In some cases, these individuals had religious or moral objections to gay rights; others were older people who had traditional values and were not comfortable with gay or lesbian lifestyles.

Over time, though, public attitudes began to change. Support for same-sex marriage rose to 35 percent in 1999, 42 percent in 2004, 46 percent in 2007, 53 percent in 2011, and 55 percent in 2014. An attitude that had begun as generally hostile to same-sex marriage in the late 1990s became one that was much more tolerant and accepting of the idea two decades later.

There were many reasons for the doubling in support for same-sex marriage. Public opinion surveys reveal a major age component to views about the subject. Whereas only 42 percent of senior citizens favored same-sex marriage, 78 percent of 18- to 29-year-olds did, as did 54 percent of those between 30 and 49 years old.[27] As elderly people passed from the scene, their place was taken by younger people who held more liberal views on many social matters.

There also were substantial differences in viewpoints based on political party and geography. Thirty percent of self-identified Republicans supported same-sex marriage, compared to 58 per-

FIGURE 3-3. *Opinions on Same-Sex Marriage, 1996–2014*

Percent in favor

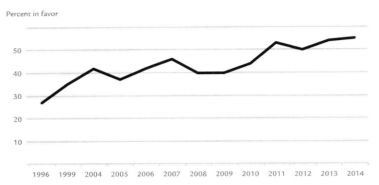

| | 1996 | 1999 | 2004 | 2005 | 2006 | 2007 | 2008 | 2009 | 2010 | 2011 | 2012 | 2013 | 2014 |

Source: Gallup Poll, "Same-Sex Marriage Support Reaches New High at 55%," May 21, 2014.

cent of independents and 74 percent of Democrats. People who live in the South are less likely (48 percent) to support same-sex marriage, compared to those who reside in the Midwest (53 percent), West (58 percent), or East (67 percent).[28]

Popular culture shifted as well. Television shows such as *Modern Family*, *Glee*, and *Law and Order* featured gay characters, and there were popular movies with gay themes or characters, such as *Brokeback Mountain*, *The Crying Game*, *Milk*, and *The Hours*.[29] What once had been marginalized in dark corners or obscure outlets now moved mainstream, enabling heterosexual people to see gays as real-life people with similar aspirations, concerns, and problems of their own.

Inevitably, money has been another factor in changing public views about homosexuality. Analysts estimate that "pink money power," the purchasing power of the gay and lesbian community, totaled $2 trillion in 2012. Jody Huckaby, the executive director of Parents, Families and Friends of Lesbians and Gays, predicted that "this economic clout and product loyalty is only going to grow. We are here to give the business world this wake-up call and to help companies compete."[30]

Over the last few years, the rapidly evolving views have led to tremendous changes in public policy at the state level. By 2015, thirty-six states had legalized same-sex marriage and others were moving in that direction when the U.S. Supreme Court struck down the Defense of Marriage Act.[31] President Obama contrasted the transformational nature of this decision with the country's usual penchant for incremental change. "Progress on this journey often comes in small increments, sometimes two steps forward, one step back, propelled by the persistent effort of dedicated citizens. And then sometimes, there are days like today, when that slow, steady effort is rewarded with justice that arrives like a thunderbolt," he said.[32]

Of course, not all states favored these developments. Places such as North Carolina, Indiana, and Arkansas gained national attention when they passed legislation weakening nondiscrimination provisions linked to sexual orientation or passing bills on such issues as which gender bathrooms transgender people should use.[33] Facing local pressure from evangelical voters unhappy with the drift of societal norms, they either dropped those clauses or provided "conscientious objection" exceptions for those who did not want to abide by those rules. Those bills were a way for people with traditional values to sidestep the broader movement toward gay, lesbian, and transgender rights.

Obamacare

Americans did something in 2008 that seemed out of character given the religious and political conservatism of the preceding three-plus decades. For the first time in its history, they elected an African American president who campaigned on a progressive agenda. This abrupt shift was made possible by an economy in shambles following the collapse of the stock market and the failure of President George W. Bush's interventionist foreign policy in Iraq, which had alienated many voters across the political spectrum. During the Great Recession, equities investors lost more than half their money and unemployment rose to double-digit levels.

Amidst this turbulent economic time, the country turned left by electing Barack Obama and gave him substantial Democratic majorities in the House and Senate. Along partisan lines, Congress passed the American Recovery and Reinvestment Act in 2009, designed to stimulate the economy, and the Patient Protection and Affordable Care Act (later known by opponents and supporters as "Obamacare") in 2010, which required people to get health insurance and provided subsidies for those unable to afford private insurance. Democrats also enacted comprehensive legislation known as Dodd-Frank (after its sponsors, Senator Christopher Dodd and Representative Barney Frank) to increase oversight and regulation of Wall Street firms widely considered responsible for the 2008 financial meltdown.

For decades, presidents and politicians had talked about health care reform. With 18 percent of Americans lacking health care insurance, many Democratic leaders had pushed universal insurance. Going back to Harry Truman and including efforts by Lyndon Johnson, Jimmy Carter, and Bill Clinton, there had been proposals to bring coverage to all, or nearly all, Americans.

All of these previous efforts failed. Politicians were not able to overcome the entropy and incrementalism that stymied change and kept more fundamental alternatives from being enacted. Interest groups invested in the status quo impeded sweeping change and advocated, instead, for a model of small-scale, incremental steps. Comprehensive decisionmaking generally went nowhere.

But President Obama was the leader who got systematic reform enacted. His legislation sought to provide near-universal health care and alter the way in which health care operates. Money was provided to modernize health care and introduce sweeping new levels of technology into the process. The idea was that improvements both in care and the health industry's business practices would increase efficiency and effectiveness and promote greater wellness for individuals. With more people having health insurance, the result would be beneficial both for them and society as a whole. It took overwhelming Democratic majorities in the House and Senate to get Obama's legislation through, but he was able to pass a bill that was a historic landmark.[34]

The legislation provoked intense reactions across the political spectrum.[35] Liberals praised the effort to cover the uninsured, although they were concerned about the compromises needed to get the legislation through Congress. Hospitals worried about their business models and whether the influx of new patients would compensate for the losses they incurred in the past for caring for the indigent. Some doctors grumbled about new requirements that they maintain electronic medical records and expressed concern about the potential impact on their relationships with patients.

But the strongest reaction came from political conservatives. They characterized the reform as a radical government takeover of American medical care. During the congressional debate, a grassroots movement known as the Tea Party emerged to challenge Obama's plan and even the validity of his entire presidency.[36] One conservative billionaire, Harold Simmons, called Obama "the most dangerous American alive" due to what Simmons said was the president's imposition of an increased role for government.[37]

Obama's health care victory came back to haunt him in the 2010 midterm elections when the Tea Party scored a major victory, with Republicans gaining sixty-three seats and taking control of the House of Representatives. Democrat Nancy Pelosi lost her speakership to Republican John Boehner, and it became virtually impossible for President Obama to push his political agenda through Congress. Thirty-two percent of Americans generally and 61 percent of Republicans considered themselves Tea Party supporters at this time, according to a Gallup poll.[38]

Although Obama was reelected president in 2012, his party suffered big losses in the 2014 midterm election. Republicans picked up thirteen seats in the House and nine seats in the Senate. The latter was the largest party switchover in several decades and enabled Republicans to regain control of the Senate.

This gave the GOP majority control both of the House and the Senate. In the last two years of his presidency, Obama had no recourse but to issue executive orders to further his policies because he was unable to get any substantive legislation through the Republican-controlled Congress. The heady days of 2009 and 2010, when they dominated the federal government, were gone for Democrats.

Income Inequality

The total assets of the super wealthy in the United States—as reported on the *Forbes* list of billionaires—have more than doubled over the past decade.[39] Ten years ago, the top 400 individuals controlled around $1 trillion; now their wealth has risen to more than $2 trillion.[40] Economists Marco Cagetti and Mariacristina De Nardi show that 1 percent of Americans now own about one-third of the country's wealth.[41]

Economists Thomas Piketty and Emmanuel Saez document how income concentration has risen over the past century. Figure 3-4 charts the share of pre-tax income accounted for by the top 1 percent of earners from 1913 to 2012.[42] In 1928, the year before the stock market crash that set off the Great Depression, that group garnered 21.1 percent of all income in the United States. Over the next fifty years, that percentage dropped to a low of 8.3 percent in 1976, then rose to 21.5 percent in 2007. It dropped to 18.8 percent in 2011 following the Great Recession, then rose again to 19.6 percent in 2012.[43] Those figures show that income concentration today is similar to what it was in the 1920s and is more than double the degree during the post–World War II period.

More detailed statistics demonstrate that after-tax income stagnated for most workers from 1979 to 2009 but rose dramatically for the top 1 percent. Charting the percent change

FIGURE 3-4. *Income Inequality, 1913–2012*

Percent of pre-tax income received by top 1 percent

Source: Thomas Piketty and Emmanuel Saez, "Income Inequality in the United States, 1913–1998," *Quarterly Journal of Economics*, vol. 118 (2003), pp. 1–39. For 1999 to 2008 numbers, see the web page of Emmanuel Saez (http://emlab.berkeley.edu/users/saez).

in real, after-tax income for four groups of workers shows that during those thirty years, earnings rose 155 percent for the top 1 percent of earners, 58 percent for the next 19 percent of earners, 45 percent for the middle 60 percent, and 37 percent for the bottom 20 percent.[44] And if Thomas Piketty, author of *Capital in the Twenty-First Century,* is correct, money is likely to become even more concentrated in the future. Drawing on data from several countries over the past 200 years, he argues that the appreciation of capital outpaces that of the economy at large and of wages in particular. That benefits the people who already hold a lot of financial resources and increases the overall concentration of wealth.[45]

Still another way to look at the income gap relies on the Gini coefficient, an economic measure developed in 1912 by Italian sociologist Corrado Gini and used to illustrate inequality in different economies. It runs from 0 to 1, with 0 indicating that everyone has the same income, and 1 showing that one person has all the income. The Gini coefficient for the United States was around .38 in 1950, dropped to .35 around 1970, and rose to .45 in 2010, demonstrating that income inequality has increased substantially over the past sixty years.[46]

As a sign of how profound income divisions have become, increasing inequality has widened the gaps among different social groups. Over the past twenty-five years, for example, the financial gulf between whites and blacks has nearly tripled. In 1984 the difference in family wealth between the races was $85,000; by 2009 it had increased to $236,500. The gaps in homeownership, education level, and financial inheritance are responsible for most of these differences; for example, according to researchers, the "home ownership rate for whites is 28 percent higher than that of blacks."[47] As Jennifer Hochschild and her collaborators at Harvard University point out, policymakers need to think seriously about the impact of these trends on social cohesion and political representation.[48]

Financial concentration has increased not just in the United States but in many other countries around the globe. Research by Thomas Piketty and Gabriel Zucman finds that wealth has risen much more rapidly than incomes in eight developed nations: Australia, Canada, France, Germany, Great Britain, Italy, Japan, and the United States. They find that "wealth-to-income ratios in these nations climbed from a range of 200 to 300 percent in 1970 to a range of 400 to 600 percent in 2010"— a doubling of the wealth concentration over that time period.[49]

The reality of inequality has generated considerable attention in many countries. In the United States, democratic socialist Bernie Sanders gained considerable traction in the 2016 nominating process by attacking billionaires and inequality in America. He argued that economic benefits flowed unfairly to the ultra-rich, as opposed to the working class, and that this was one of the reasons why economic growth lagged behind previous eras. More government programs need to be provided to people of average means through free college and a single payer health system so that they can make a better future for themselves, Sanders maintained.

Looking at the world as a whole, the United Nations World Institute for Development Economics Research showed that in 2008, the top 1 percent of earners owned a total of 40.1 percent of overall global wealth, a share that is larger than the one-third of national wealth owned by the top 1 percent in the United States.[50] Overall, the Gini coefficient for global income has increased substantially over the past two centuries. According to World Bank economist Branko Milanovic, inequality rose from .43 percent in 1820, to .53 in 1850, and .56 in 1870, continuing to rise in the new century to .61 percent in 1913, .62 in 1929, .64 in 1960, .66 in 1980, and .71 in 2002.[51]

Trumpism and Border Security

In recent years the open flow of people across national boundaries has spawned a backlash from those worried about jobs, national sovereignty, terrorism, and cultural values. Within the United States, there have been calls to build a wall along the country's southern border with Mexico to keep out undocumented (or "illegal") immigrants. Popularized by Republican presidential candidate Donald Trump, this rhetoric speaks to concerns about border security and rising fears about the geographic integrity of the United States. If the country cannot protect its own borders during a period of threats from abroad, the argument goes, what does it mean to be an American and how can a nation deal with adversaries?

Moves to the right on policy issues are not unusual during periods following financial crises. According to economists Manuel Funke, Moritz Schularick, and Christoph Trebesch, an analysis of such crises over the past 140 years shows that "policy uncertainty rises strongly after financial crises as government majorities shrink and polarization rises. After a crisis, voters seem to be particularly attracted to the political rhetoric of the extreme right, which often attributes blame to minorities or foreigners." These researchers go on to note that "far-right parties increase their vote share by 30% after a financial crisis."[52]

Conservative leaders have linked the issues of a stagnant economy and border security to Mexican immigrants, trade unfairness with China, and diminished fortunes for middle-class workers. According to their reasoning, border problems are symptomatic of more general problems plaguing Western countries. The unfettered flow of immigrants raises questions about national identity, domestic security, and economic well-being for the country as a whole. Having a weak grip on cross-border population flows diminishes nations' abilities to guide their own futures, according to this view.

Concern over border security has become a major political issue in Europe as well. As many countries have grappled with the crisis of refugees from Syria, North Africa, and Afghanistan, they have clamped down on immigrants and beefed up their border security. Hungary, Austria, and Macedonia have built fences or walls and closed off portions of their borders. Others, such as Denmark, have toughened their rules regarding who is eligible to come to their countries and be reunited with family members.

In the United States, Trump gained popular support through his tough stance on immigration and harsh tone toward those who disagree with him. This especially was the case following terrorist attacks in San Bernardino, California, in 2015 and Orlando, Florida, in 2016. Using strong positions on the border and strident comments about Muslims, the Republican presidential candidate surprised the experts with his substantial public support.

News coverage played into Trump's hands throughout the campaign. According to commentator Norman Ornstein, "Nearly every Trump rally is covered in real time; every outrageous Trump statement or action gets blanket attention."[53] This seemingly nonstop outpouring of media reporting helped Trump dominate news coverage during the months leading into the 2016 election. Analysis of coverage found that Trump got many more times the newspaper coverage and television time than any of his competitors.

In analyzing his appeal to some voters, social scientists found a clear streak of authoritarianism among them. Those who favored Trump liked the tough and uncompromising stances he took on many issues. Researcher Matthew MacWilliams analyzed public opinion data and concluded that "authoritarians obey. They rally to and follow strong leaders. And they respond aggressively to outsiders, especially when they feel threatened."[54]

Opinion data from other countries furthermore documented a tie between support for right-wing politicians and economic anxieties unleashed by free trade and globalization. Relying on in-depth analysis of polling information, researchers demonstrated, in a paper for the National Bureau of Economic Research, that "the economic frustrations of trade nudged many people into becoming right-wing extremists over the past two decades." In an argument consistent with a megachange interpretation, the researchers found that the economic forces generated by globalization radicalized voters and produced "the largest increases in support for far-right parties."[55]

Some observers have gone even further in saying that Trump represents the opening wedge of fascism in America. Writer Ezra Klein openly worries about an "ideology of violence" that permeates Trump's campaign. Anti-Trump protesters have been threatened and punched, while the candidate himself incited his followers to "knock the hell out of them. I promise you I will pay for the legal fees."[56] Not surprisingly, given the intense confrontations between Trump supporters and opponents, violence flared at several of the candidate's rallies. Protesters were punched and spat on as they were removed physically from a number of events.[57]

Brookings Institution Senior Fellow Robert Kagan claims that Trump represents a dangerous blend of toughness along with racial and ethnic hatred. "What he offers is an attitude, an aura of crude strength and machismo, a boasting disrespect for the niceties of the democratic culture that he claims, and his followers believe, has produced national weakness and incompetence. His incoherent and contradictory utterances have one thing in common: They provoke and play on feelings of resentment and disdain, intermingled with bits of fear, hatred and anger. His public discourse consists of attacking or ridiculing a wide range of 'others'—Muslims, Hispanics, women, Chinese, Mexicans, Europeans, Arabs, immigrants, refugees—whom he depicts either as threats or as objects of derision."[58]

During a period of considerable social and economic flux,

there are many sources of discontent. Middle-class workers feel their jobs are threatened by multinational corporations "outsourcing" work to workers in other countries and by immigrants willing to work for substandard wages. The combination of the perceived threat from abroad and increased employment competition at home appears to be a major driver of political support for ultra-nationalist politicians. Voter anger and anxiety is higher today than in many years and appears closely linked to the rise of self-described "strong" leaders who talk tough on immigrants, refugees, and border security.

There is a significant association between terrorism and a political turn to the right both in Europe and the United States. Trump himself pinpointed the link between the anxiety unleashed by terrorist attacks and his own following. When discussing his electoral support, he said, "Paris happened. . . . All of a sudden the poll numbers just shot up."[59] The billionaire understood that when voters felt under siege, they become more likely to favor strident language and aggressive policies against perceived threats, notably Muslims and immigrants. His sharp rhetoric pushed America further than it had gone in many decades toward machismo politics and illiberal democracy.[60]

The Rapid Pace of Domestic Change

The past few decades have produced major alterations in domestic opinion and public policy. Topics such as religion, taxes, government spending, marijuana use, same-sex marriage, health care, income inequality, and border control have gone through substantial shifts in public opinion and—on some of those topics—also in actual policy.

In some cases, a catalytic election led to shifts in public policy. For example, the elections of 1980, 1994, and 2000 were especially crucial in moving the United States to the right, while the 2008 election shifted national life temporarily to the left. In other cases, public policy moved because of grassroots changes percolating through American society. Changes in same-sex marriage and marijuana legalization, as an illustration, were driven less by electoral results than by broader social changes in the country at large. The resurgence of public concern over border security has been led by nationalistic politicians and media coverage about the dangers of terrorism, crime, and disease emanating from abroad. Sometimes, global developments have fed into domestic policymaking and highlighted particular threats to the United States.

Looking over the entire time span of recent decades, the various transformations took place in multifaceted directions. In the 1980s social reactions to changes in the 1960s and 1970s, coupled with political changes as part of the Reagan revolution, moved the country in a conservative direction. However, that transformation gave way to societal changes that shifted the culture in a liberal direction, such as seen in the cases of same-sex marriage and marijuana legalization. In recent years, though, many voters became worried about globalization, border security, and apparent threats at home and abroad, and those concerns have moved parts of the U.S. agenda toward a more nationalistic perspective. These sentiments stopped comprehensive immigration reform from taking place and led Congress to increase resources on national security and border protection.

In many respects, dramatic change has become the new constant of American politics, even when the specific policy stances have shifted from conservative to liberal and then to nationalistic. Indeed, multifaceted change is a hallmark of recent years. Shifts in one direction can mobilize opponents, and plant the seeds of a counter-movement. That helps to explain how the United States gets large-scale change of differing complexions. It is hard for any single social or political force to dominate for an extended period of time.

CHAPTER 4

Thermidorian Reactions

In 1794 French revolutionary leader Maximilien Robespierre was arrested and executed along with many of his top advisers. Just one year before, these Jacobin politicians had sent King Louis XVI to the guillotine, abolished slavery, and ended feudal privileges in France. Instilled with populist and democratic fervor, they and their followers at the Committee of Public Safety had unleashed a "Reign of Terror" that resulted in the execution of thousands of the deposed king's loyalists.[1]

However, the excesses of this group spawned a counterrevolution that led to its own demise. Soon after they executed the French monarch, nearly two dozen of them were killed summarily without trial by opponents. Leaders from the National Convention seized control of the government and ushered in what came to be called the Thermidorian Convention. Historians refer to this countercoup as a Thermidorian reaction that moved the revolution in a radically different direction.[2]

Befitting the period of great turmoil in revolutionary France, the Thermidorian Convention lasted only five years before Napoleon Bonaparte seized control in a military coup. This era of coup, followed by countercoup, and then a military dicta-torship illustrates that periods of megachange often spawn counterrevolutions that move in unanticipated ways. Given their intrinsic chaos, revolutions rarely move in a smooth or consistent direction.

In this chapter, I look at several examples of what might be called Thermidorian reactions in more recent times. They include the 1960s liberal protests that spawned conservative reactions, alterations in views about tobacco smoking, shifts in sentiments concerning the HIV/AIDS virus, the Catholic Church's shift from Popes John Paul II and Benedict XVI to Pope Francis, and the establishment of U.S. diplomatic rela-tions with Cuba. I demonstrate why in a period of megachange there can be fluctuations from one side to another. Even when there are dramatic shifts, revolutions are incomplete and some-times contain the seeds of their own demise.

How 1960s Protests Spawned Conservative Reactions

In the period following World War II, the United States basked in the goodwill resulting from that international triumph. At home, the economy grew rapidly and the middle class pros-pered. Politics functioned, for the most part, in the center of the ideological spectrum, and bargaining, compromise, and negotiation ensured that most changes were incremental.

Starting in the 1960s and thereafter, though, the momen-tum for major change accelerated. The civil rights movement began to build to a dramatic crescendo. Martin Luther King Jr. attracted extraordinary attention with his "I Have a Dream" speech in Washington, D.C., in 1963. Arguing for a land where African Americans could have justice and enjoy the same op-portunities as whites, King received rave reviews for his uplift-ing rhetoric. The media and public attention generated by that mass demonstration helped lay the groundwork for major civil rights and voting rights legislation in following years.[3]

By the late-1960s, opposition to the Vietnam War surged and grassroots activists built a strong antiwar movement. Young people, in particular, did not understand why America had sent tens of thousands of troops to this war on the other side of the globe. The conflict seemed just one more sign of a government that was out of touch with morality and good political judgment.

To combat the military escalation, they marched on Washington, organized local protests on college campuses, took over campus administrative buildings, and attempted to increase public antipathy against the war.[4] While they were not successful at ending the war right away, they did produce substantial changes in higher education. Faced with students who wanted greater freedom, many universities ended their "in loco parentis" restrictions on individual behavior, built co-ed dorms, and liberalized curricular requirements.[5]

Around the same time, women were becoming increasingly willing to challenge their own inequitable treatment. Leaders such as Gloria Steinem, Bella Abzug, and Betty Friedan spoke out strongly against injustice. They complained about discrimination and prejudice and fought to enact antidiscrimination legislation. Similar to the suffragettes of decades earlier, they endured ridicule from adversaries and struggled to build political support for the cause of "women's liberation."

In 1972 they succeeded in getting Congress to approve the Equal Rights Amendment to the Constitution. With its overall goal of equal rights for women, the proposed amendment set off a raucous debate about everything from employment and wages to bathrooms. Although it was ratified by thirty-five states, the proposed amendment failed to meet the three-quarters threshold (thirty-eight states) to be added to the Constitution, and therefore was not approved.[6]

Each of these social movements achieved certain successes for minorities, young people, and women. Adherents were able to mount pressure for new laws, reform institutions, and generate changes in attitudes and behavior. Social and political processes were opened up and opportunities provided for career advancement for marginalized populations.

Yet the 1960s protests generated a cultural and political counter-reaction that would last for decades. Typical of Thermidorian reactions, the rise of countercultures threatens mainstream elements and leads to efforts to move society back to where it had been. The 1960s ended with politicians such as Richard Nixon mobilizing what he called the "silent majority" to push a very different agenda.[7]

Conservatives then, and now, worried about lifestyle changes associated with the protest movements of the 1960s. They saw drug use and sexual promiscuity among young people as dangerous to the longterm health of society. They also worried about an activist federal government pushing social and political change on parts of society that did not support equal rights for women or civil rights for racial minorities. According to historian Stephen Prothero, "Culture wars have been conservative projects, instigated and waged by people anxious about the loss of old orders and the emergence of new ones."[8]

Sensing a backlash from streets protests, urban riots, and uncertainty over cultural liberalization, politicians such as Nixon and Ronald Reagan argued the country was moving in the wrong direction and America needed order and stability in the face of chaos and tumultuous change. Each of these leaders would position himself as being a bulwark against the excesses of the 1960s.[9]

These and similar appeals substantially altered the political dialogue. For several decades, Republicans more often than not would control major elective institutions nationally and, increasingly, in a majority of states. Their message of social conservatism and limited government would resonate with many voters and dominate the civic discourse of the country. While parts of society would continue to liberalize in line with 1960s sentiments, notably in terms of lifestyle choices, conservative political leaders found the greatest success when they promised to cut taxes, reduce government regulations and waste, and crack down on "welfare cheats" and others said to be relying too heavily on government support. Despite the progressive inclinations of the 1960s, these elected officials moved national policy in a more conservative direction.

Decades later, a national survey showed the deep partisan differences unleashed by the cultural changes of the 1960s. When asked in 2013 whether American culture was better today or in the 1950s, 59 percent of Democrats thought it was better today, compared to 31 percent of Republicans and just 22 percent of Tea Party identifiers.[10] Befitting an era of cultural transformation, people from various viewpoints displayed differing assessments of these changes.

Antismoking Attitudes and Policies

Well into the 1960s, smoking was widely accepted in America and public policies allowed people to smoke wherever they wanted. This included airplanes, workplaces, bars, and restaurants. It was common for people on television and in movies to smoke and, supposedly, to be "cool" and sophisticated. There was nothing unusual about people lighting up a cigarette in public places. Tobacco companies marketed "slim" cigarettes for women to encourage them to smoke.

Yet things started to change when scientific research suggested there were health hazards associated with smoking. For the first time in 1964, a U.S. surgeon general's report argued there was a connection between smoking and several different diseases. In that publication, Luther Terry claimed that exposure to chemicals in smoke raised the risk of cancer and heart disease and, therefore, could be fatal to smokers or those around them.[11]

Faced with growing evidence of health risks, Congress passed the Federal Cigarette Labeling and Advertising Act of 1965. It required a health warning on cigarette packages, mandated an annual report on smoking and health, and banned broadcast ads of cigarettes.[12] In 1988 an amendment to the Federal Aviation Act outlawed smoking on domestic flights lasting fewer than two hours. Twelve years later, federal legislation broadened that prohibition to all flights running between the United States and foreign airports.[13]

Starting in the late 1980s in major cities, then gradually across the country, states and localities banned smoking in workplaces, restaurants, and bars to shield nonsmokers from health risks. Many of these jurisdictions also placed limits on advertising and sales, especially to children under the age of 18.[14] Around 100 cities (such as New York City and Needham, Massachusetts) and the state of Hawaii raised the minimum age for buying tobacco products to 21.[15]

Accompanying these policy changes were dramatic shifts in public behavior and citizen opinion. As shown in figure 4-1, the percentage of Americans who told Gallup that they smoke dropped from a high of 45 percent in 1955 to 21 percent in 2014.[16] That reduction represented one of the greatest alterations in personal health behavior in many years. It generally is difficult for people to alter their individual behavior—especially when it involves addictive behavior—yet tobacco smoking is an area where this actually has happened due to health concerns, peer pressure, and even public policy.

These changes in personal behavior were accompanied, possibly even influenced, by substantial changes in public preferences about tobacco smoking. Even at the height of smoking

FIGURE 4-1. *Smokers, 1944–2014*

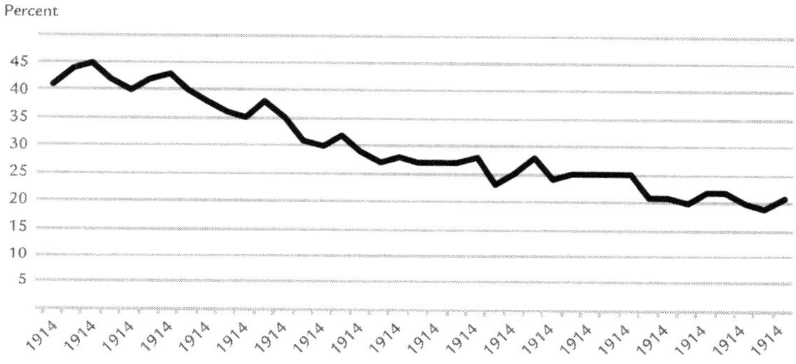

Percent

Source: Gallup Poll, "Tobacco and Smoking," April 8, 2015.

popularity, a majority of Americans did not smoke, so it is no surprise that nonsmokers were an influential force. For example, the percentage of people who said smoking in public places should be made illegal rose from 31 percent in 2003 to 56 percent in 2014 (see figure 4-2). That is nearly a doubling in the percentage taking a tough stance on this policy issue.

Many of these antismoking policies also became increasingly common in other countries. There were smoking crackdowns in much of Europe, Latin America, Australia and New Zealand, the Caribbean, and parts of Asia and Africa (though antismoking policies were difficult to implement in places like China and Russia that still had strong smoking cultures). Limitations on smoking were enacted even in countries such as France and Indonesia, where smoking has been glorified and where significant local companies had marketed cigarettes.[17] Many of these moves involved restrictions on smoking in workplaces, restaurants, and public gathering places. Even Parisian restaurants and cafés today, long seen as the epitome of the smoking culture, have no smoking areas.

FIGURE 4-2. *Opinions on Smoking in Public Places, 2001–14*

Percent who favor banning

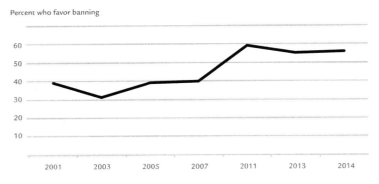

Source: Gallup Poll, "Tobacco and Smoking," April 8, 2015.

HIV and AIDS

In the early 1980s, the human immunodeficiency virus (HIV), that came to be known as AIDS (autoimmune deficiency syndrome), was widely thought to afflict primarily homosexual men and therefore was considered unimportant and non-threatening to the wider society. Since it was a sickness of a marginalized community, the federal government spent very little money to understand the disease and even less on treatment and prevention. Even as a deadly epidemic unfolded, the Reagan administration did virtually nothing to deal with this emerging health crisis.

But in 1984, a small-town Indiana boy named Ryan White, suffering from hemophilia, contracted the illness after receiving a blood transfusion. He attracted national attention when his suburban middle school in Kokomo refused to let him attend classes, despite the minimal health risks he posed to other children. With very little understanding of how the disease spread, the community vehemently opposed having him sit in classrooms with other pupils.

This unfair action by the school generated a tremendous amount of media coverage around the country and stimulated considerable conversation about how the disease spread and who was being affected. Through the lens of an innocent young boy who by chance was drawn into the news vortex, the incident launched a national conversation and broadened people's understanding of the disease. It became a teaching moment on a grand scale and fundamentally altered how people understood the transmission and treatment of AIDS.

Greater dialogue and more federal funding came when celebrities such as basketball player Magic Johnson, actor Rock Hudson, and tennis star Arthur Ashe contracted HIV. In 1981 the federal government provided around $200 million in funding for research into HIV; that level went up during the 1980s and reached $1.3 billion in 1989.[18]

In 1990, nearly six years after the outpouring of media coverage of the Hoosier student and the year of his death, Congress passed the Ryan White Care Act, which offered additional funding for people suffering from the illness. As shown on figure 4-3, federal funding reached $2.7 billion in 1995, $4.5 billion in 2000, $6.3 billion in 2005, and $6.6 billion in 2009.[19]

The spurt of government funding fundamentally turned around treatment of the illness. According to gay rights activist Larry Kramer, "Ryan White probably did more to change the face of this illness and to move people than anyone.[20] His personal courage and individual suffering led to a shift in public policy and better understanding of the disease.

Interestingly, as federal funding increased, public concern about AIDS declined. Figure 4-4 shows the percentage of Americans citing AIDS as the most urgent health problem facing the country. In 1987, 68 percent named it, but this percentage dropped to 49 percent in 1990, 17 percent in 2002, and 7 percent in 2011.[21]

One explanation for this decline might be that, over time,

FIGURE 4-3. *Federal Funding for HIV/AIDS, 1981–2009*

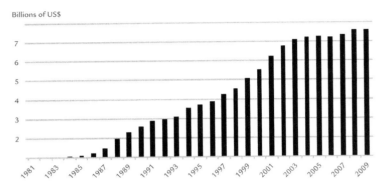

Billions of US$

Source: Judith Johnson, "AIDS Funding for Federal Government Programs: FY1981–FY2009," April 23, 2008, Congressional Research Service.

FIGURE 4-4. *AIDS as Urgent Health Problem, 1987–2011*

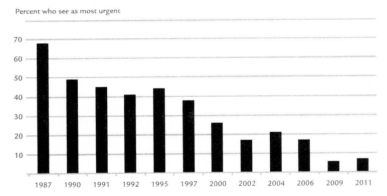

Percent who see as most urgent

Source: Kaiser Family Foundation, "HIV/AIDS at 30: A Public Opinion Perspective," June 2011, p. 3.

the general public learned more about the disease and therefore became more comfortable in dealing with those suffering from HIV/AIDS. In 1997 the Gallup organization asked whether people felt comfortable working with someone who had HIV/ AIDS and only 32 percent indicated they did. By 2011, though, nearly half (49 percent) said they felt comfortable, demonstrating a significant improvement in how people reacted to the illness.[22]

Both in terms of public opinion and federal funding, then, public reaction to HIV/AIDS illustrates how major shifts can arise from small beginnings. If personal stories encapsulate larger points—especially when the personal stories involve sympathetic characters—change can become bigger than those particular individuals. Media coverage can dramatize certain aspects and affect how people perceive reality. A series of human stories sometimes can be very powerful in altering narratives and affecting the course of history.

Pope John Paul II, Pope Benedict XVI, and Pope Francis

Thermidorian reactions do not just unfold in the political realm, but in civil society as well. In the late 1950s and early 1960s, for example, the Catholic Church attempted to modernize its practices in response to social change around the world. Led by Pope John XXIII, church leaders opened the Second Vatican Council and sought to bring religious practices more in line with contemporary life.[23] The council made a number of important decisions, notably allowing masses to be conducted in native languages, as opposed to only in Latin. It also reiterated the importance of equality before God and the human rights of all people and sought to reconcile with other faiths where relations had been broken.

Yet those efforts turned out to be a short interlude in an enduring conservative trend. Subsequent pontiffs, such as John Paul II and Benedict XVI, resisted additional reforms and pushed the church sharply back in the direction of doctrinal purity. They took a tough stance against abortion, the use of contraceptives, divorce, gay and lesbian lifestyles, premarital sex, and secularization in general. Pope John Paul II, a native of Poland, also took an uncompromising stance against communism. Having endured the pain of living under an authoritarian regime since after World War II, he preached against communism and advocated for greater liberty and freedom. He also argued that Western liberal positions on abortion and, increasingly, euthanasia, violated the sanctity of life. Although many Catholics wished to liberalize church practices regarding the ordination of women and homosexuality, Pope John Paul II whole-heartedly opposed these efforts and endorsed long-standing church policies in these areas.[24]

Benedict XVI had been the doctrinal enforcer for his predecessor, and he continued to push the church in a conservative direction on doctrinal issues when he became pope in 2005. He decried "moral relativism" and secularization, and he insisted that the church must remain an ethical beacon even if its practices conflicted with modern opinions. He even talked about the value of Latin in religious services, something the church had largely dropped in the early 1960s.

However, Benedict's papacy did not end well. The church was roiled by complaints about financial mismanagement and fierce criticism of how it handled charges of sexual abuse by priests, primarily against young boys. Critics argued that Pope Benedict did not take firm enough action against this behavior and, in some cases, overlooked transgressions about which he had been informed. Amid the criticism, Benedict in 2013 took the unusual step of announcing his retirement on grounds that poor health made it impossible for him to fulfill his papal duties. He became one of the few popes to leave his post voluntarily.

Following Benedict's retirement, the College of Cardinals chose Jorge Mario Bergoglio of Argentina as the new leader. He chose the name Pope Francis, in honor of Saint Francis of Assisi. Unhappy with financial management by the Vatican Bank and concerned about underrepresentation in church leadership of the developing world, he moved to liberalize church practices and broaden social and economic inclusion.[25] He condemned priestly sex abuses and spoke of the importance of pastoral care for the poor and needy. In contrast to his predecessors, he met with progressive priests and beatified Archbishop Oscar Romero, a liberal church leader who had been assassinated in El Salvador in 1980 for taking a strong position on the side of the downtrodden.[26]

Pope Francis was sensitive to the disadvantaged and said the church should focus more on pastoral care of all people, regardless of whether they accepted all aspects of its doctrine. This led him to adopt more inclusive language on homosexuality and the role of women in the church. Seeking to make sure that his approach would outlive his own papacy, he named many new cardinals, most of whom came from the developing world. He seemed to hope that these moves would ensure that the next pope and future doctrinal decisions would rest on principles of social justice and inclusion.

Pope Francis also has called for new discussions within the church regarding social and economic change. At a 2014 Synod on the Family, he asked people to talk openly "without fear." *Washington Post* columnist Michael Gerson said that the pope has "a pastoral passion to meet people where they are—to recognize some good, even in their brokenness, and to call them to something better. That something better is not membership in a stable institution, or even the comforts of ethical religion; it is a relationship with Jesus, from which all else follows."[27]

In 2015 Francis issued a widely read encyclical about climate change, environmental degradation, and social justice. Theologian John Zizioulas, who spoke at the pope's press conference, proclaimed that "the ecological crisis is essentially a spiritual problem. The proper relationship between humanity and earth has been broken by the fall, both outwardly and within us. This rupture constitutes what we call sin. The church must introduce in its teaching the sin against the environment. The ecological sin."[28]

Pope Francis emphasized this theme in a 2015 speech at the United Nations. "Any harm done to the environment, therefore, is harm done to humanity," he said. "A selfish and boundless thirst for power and material prosperity leads both to the misuse of available natural resources and to the exclusion of the weak and the disadvantaged."[29]

After a visit to the border between Mexico and the United States, the pope talked about the plight of immigrants and the dangers of building a wall between the two countries. Asked by a reporter about GOP candidate Donald Trump's plan to construct such a wall, Pope Francis said that this would not be something that a Christian person would support.[30]

In 2016 the pope even sought to adapt to changing family life by welcoming divorced Catholics to the holy sacraments. In a lengthy treatise called *Amoris Laetitia* ("The Joy of Love"), he asked religious leaders to be open to divorced individuals, single parents, and unmarried couples. "A pastor cannot feel that it is enough to simply apply moral laws to those living in 'irregular' situations as if they were stones to throw at people's lives," he argued. Instead, priests should welcome them to the church and allow them to take communion.[31]

Despite sharp attacks on some of his pronouncements, the pontiff has explained why it is important to "heal the wounds" within the church. He sought to avoid turning faith into an ideological battle. Rather than fight doctrinal wars, he worried that wars over faith merely drive people away from religion and close doors between people. His goal was to keep dialogue open even if there were disagreements over fundamental issues.[32]

The result of his leadership has been a church that has liberalized in several important respects. Pope Francis has encouraged people to revisit doctrinal issues and make sure that religious disagreements do not interfere with pastoral care. Even if priests and parishioners cannot agree on church matters, he does not want that to create schisms within the faith or exclude people from religious participation. His goal is to build a big tent under which a diverse set of Catholics can worship and pursue their personal faith with God.

Not everyone within the church, of course, has accepted this new direction. Some religious conservatives attacked the pope's message and said they would resist his alterations. For example, Cardinal Raymond Burke of Wisconsin argued that papal power "is not absolute. . . . The pope does not have the power to change teaching [or] doctrine." Bishop Thomas Tobin of Rhode Island complained that "in trying to accommodate the needs of the age, as Pope Francis suggests, the church risks the danger of losing its courageous, countercultural, prophetic voice—one that the world needs to hear."[33] Despite these criticisms, though, the Catholic leader put the church on a very different course from his predecessors.

Recognizing Cuba

Ever since the Cuban Revolution in 1959, American policy has ostracized that Caribbean nation and cut off diplomatic ties. The justification centered on cold war politics and not wanting the Soviet Union to gain a foothold ninety miles from the southern tip of Florida. America even tried a military invasion at the Bay of Pigs, but was never able to dislodge the Fidel Castro regime.

Communism collapsed in Russia and throughout Eastern Europe between 1989 and 1991, yet the American embargo on trade and official communication with Cuba endured. The hope was that isolating the small country economically and focusing on its human rights abuses eventually would bring the Castro regime to its knees. Congressional leaders were relentless in their criticism of Cuba and the government's authoritarian practices.

By the twenty-first century, though, five decades of embargoes, isolation, and diplomatic pressure had not been successful.

Cuban leaders Fidel and Raul Castro outlasted ten American presidents and demonstrated their country could endure tough economic and political sanctions. In that situation, the time seemed ripe for a new approach.

President Obama met with Cuban President Raul Castro in 2015 during a session of the United Nations in New York City. This was the first official meeting between Cuban and American heads of state in more than half a century. As a small first step, Cuba attended the Summit of the Americas that year. "The United States will not be imprisoned by the past—we're looking to the future," Obama said. "I'm not interested in having battles that frankly started before I was born. The cold war has been over for a long time."[34]

Obama took Cuba off the State Department's list of state-sponsored terrorism and called for Congress to lift the trade embargo on Cuba and limits on travel to the Caribbean nation. The president opened a U.S. embassy in Havana and encouraged cultural and educational exchanges between the two countries. In 2016 he visited Cuba, becoming the first sitting president to do so since Calvin Coolidge's visit in 1928 for a pan-American conference.

Despite the long U.S. boycott of Cuba, American public opinion toward Cuba had improved dramatically in recent years. When asked about favorability toward that country, public sentiment shifted from only 10 percent favorable in 1996 to 46 percent favorable in 2015 (see figure 4-5).[35] This represented a major change in public attitudes and helped to explain why it was a good time for President Obama to open the door to recognizing Cuba.

There also were significant generational changes. For years, many leaders of the anti-Castro community in the United States—especially in south Florida—were actual immigrants from the island. They took a hard-line toward the Castros and exercised great influence in Congress. The next generation,

FIGURE 4-5. *Views of Cuba, 1996–2015*

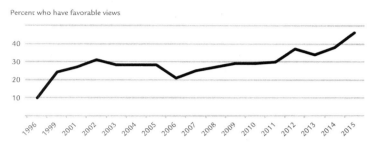

Percent who have favorable views

Source: Gallup Poll, "Attitudes Towards Cuba," April 20, 2015.

however, was more willing to admit that U.S. policy had failed. Obama was able to act because Congress no longer was hostage to a unified anti-Castro Cuban-American lobby.

These shifts in public opinion laid the groundwork for new thinking on Cuban policy. A growing number of Americans understood that the old policy had been ineffective and that new approaches were required. Although many Republican leaders condemned Obama's policy shift and refused to remove the trade embargo, Americans began the process of embracing the new policy.

Thesis and Antithesis

In his classic trilogy of thesis, antithesis, and synthesis, famed philosopher Georg Wilhelm Hegel noted that history can take big swings from one extreme to another.[36] Human events often start out in one direction but stimulate very different reactions. Out of the composite of these conflicting tendencies comes a grand synthesis that unites earlier thinking into a new approach.

That description may work well when describing intellectual tendencies, but it is not clear how the dynamic plays out in the worlds of sectarian conflict and geopolitical tension. As has been true throughout much of history, the big forces that move domestic politics and global affairs are economics, religion, politics, and armed aggression. One of the reasons we have a chaotic and unpredictable world is the difficulty of producing a grand synthesis that reconciles previous divisions over these matters.

It is common today, during a period of polarization and extremism, for one side to want to conquer if not obliterate the other. Polar opposites fight to the death and are not able or willing to negotiate their differences. Instead, they go all-out to vanquish their opponent(s) in order to gain total victory. This raises the stakes of political and economic conflict and creates extraordinary tension for all involved.

With the difficulties of generating a synthesis and the high stakes of the competition, too many contestants have little incentive to compromise, and a number of them push their activism to the extreme. This makes everyone anxious because it leads to a winner-take-all mentality with a few winners and many losers. This is the risk whether one is talking about economics, politics, or religious conflict.

Megachange elevates the scale and intensity of competition, and therefore complicates problem resolution. We need to figure out ways to break down this winner-take-all competition and produce outcomes that help a wide variety of contestants. If leaders are not able to do that, resolving disagreements will be impossible.

CHAPTER 5

The Complications of Zealotry

In 1965 theologian Harvey Cox attracted considerable attention when he wrote *The Secular City: Secularization and Urbanization in Theological Perspective*.[1] In it, Cox argued that "the rise of urban civilization and the collapse of traditional religion are the two main hallmarks of our era." As society secularized, Cox claimed, religion would become less central to people's thinking and exercise less power over social and political life.

Cox clearly was correct that the world would modernize and grow more secular and interconnected. In an era of globalization, modernization has spread around the globe. Starbucks cafés, urban malls, and McDonald's fast-food restaurants are found in nearly every corner of the world. Billions of people have access to instantaneous communications with individuals and businesses that are thousands of miles away, and they buy products from around the world.

Yet increased communications and trade have not weakened the power of religion. Instead, with the growth of very conservative, or "fundamentalist," strains of Christianity, Islam, and Judaism (plus some elements of Hinduism), religious sentiment has intensified in many places. The disorder of the current world exacerbates social tensions by making people anxious about megachange and by driving some individuals back to traditional values. They take solace in time-worn orthodoxies regarding ways to think about moral values and social relationships.

The conflict over religion and morality takes different forms around the world. The Christian fundamentalist in the United States who supports "creationism" and denies the reality of climate change is different from the ultra-Orthodox Jew in Israel who demands that his fellow countrymen and women conform to his own beliefs. In turn, each of these believers differs considerably from a Muslim suicide bomber in Iraq who kills innocent civilians in the name of Islam and practices medieval forms of male domination over women.

But in each of these societies, religious fervor and intolerance complicate the ability of leaders to resolve social, economic, and political controversies. Regardless of whether one is talking about America, France, the United Kingdom, Israel, Afghanistan, Iraq, or other places around the Middle East, many countries have witnessed sharp and sometimes violent conflicts over religion, culture, and personal lifestyles. Megachange, when combined with political extremism and strong religious sentiment, creates a volatile societal mix that can roil elections and governance. This is apparent in the domestic politics as well as in international affairs of many nations.

In the United States, for example, conservative religious beliefs have led to intense arguments with moderates and liberals over the teaching of evolution and creationism in the classroom, Middle East foreign policy, the acceptance of gay lifestyles, and, more recently, transgender use of bathrooms. In Israel major confrontations occur between Orthodox and non-Orthodox Jews about education, bus lines, housing settlements, and foreign policy. In a number of Arab countries, radical Muslims disagree with secularists over the role of women, religious doctrines, and nearly every aspect of public policy; in addition, age-old religious tensions between Sunnis and Shiites have exploded, and the resulting conflict has turned violent.

In this chapter, I look at how strong religious sentiment fuels political extremism and megachange in various places around the world. I argue that disagreements over religion and moral values have impeded conflict resolution and led to seemingly irresolvable arguments. Having strongly held beliefs, along with a refusal to concede the legitimacy of opposing views, has intensified contemporary disputes over politics, society, and religion—making compromise difficult or even impossible. There also is a significant interaction between domestic and international affairs. When partisans in one community see extreme actions in another, they use that to justify strong responses on their own part. The result is a perpetual cycle of conflict, violence, and radicalism.

The Clashes between and within Civilizations

According to the Pew-Templeton Global Religious Futures Project, Christianity was the world's most popular religion in 2010 with 2.2 billion believers, while Islam was a distant second with 1.6 billion adherents. However, by 2050 Islam is projected to have 2.8 billion followers, almost on par with Christianity at 2.9 billion adherents. In Europe 10 percent of the population will be Muslim. And in the United States, Islam likely will replace Judaism as the largest non-Christian religion.[2]

The question is what impact these changing numbers will have on domestic and global affairs. In his controversial 1996 book, *The Clash of Civilization*, Harvard political scientist Sam Huntington claimed that the big divide in the modern era is between civilizations with diverging religions, values, and perceptions about morality. According to Huntington, "The fundamental source of conflict in this new world will not be primarily ideological or primarily economic. The great divisions among humankind and the dominating source of conflict will be cultural."[3] From this standpoint, much of the enmity people feel toward one another centers on differing views regarding culture and morality.

Considerable evidence has mounted in subsequent years to support that viewpoint. Common secular norms of individual freedom, equity for women, and reduced emphasis on organized religion in much of the West have run headlong into principles grounded almost exclusively on faith-based perspectives. That is particularly apparent in the Middle East where, for example, the Islamic State of Iraq and Syria forces have crucified or beheaded Christians or harmed Shiites or Sunnis who don't accept their interpretations of Islam.

The fast pace of change makes many people uncomfortable, anxious, or angry. Some people refuse to tolerate or even attempt to understand those who have different backgrounds or views. Others think they are the true believers and everyone else has false views or simply is misguided.

Writer Michael Walzer argues that the "paradox of liberation" is that religions with a goal of personal empowerment often end up taking authoritarian and ultra-orthodox forms. "Raising consciousness is a persuasive enterprise, but it quickly turns into a cultural war between the liberators and what we can call the traditionalists."[4] In some places, the end result has been religious-based regimes that are intolerant of alternative points of view and penalize those with conflicting values.

In the modern world, though, it is not just a question of clashes between civilizations. There also are important conflicts *within* civilizations. Historically and up to the present day, each of the world's major monotheistic religions has faced intense fights within the community over the proper relationship between religion and politics, primarily over the question of whether, and to what extent, religious doctrine should influence public policy. Sometimes, the tug-of-war within religious communities is as intense as that across cultures. Especially in a period of megachange, basic disagreements over faith and values can have important consequences for politics and society in general, not just individual religions and their adherents.

A Visit to Lebanon

In some of my travels, I have seen the conflicts between secularization and traditional values up close. During a 2004 trip, I met a 23-year-old Lebanese woman who had grown up in Jounieh, a coastal city just north of Beirut, under a very strict father. Following Middle Eastern customs, he insisted she not go out by herself or spend time with her boyfriend alone. Her mother and close friends, though, helped her evade these rules by going out with her under the guise they were going to the same place. Then the mother (or friend) would go elsewhere and the young lady would be free to spend time with the boyfriend. After the visit, she would call her mother on a cell phone (which her father did not know she had), rendezvous with her, and the two would go home as if they had spent the afternoon together.

Such is the environment in which many Middle Eastern women are forced to live because of the harsh rules pushed by males within the family and the overall community. It was fascinating that the mother and daughter formed a premeditated conspiracy against the family patriarch. They worked together to create personal space for themselves in the midst of tight social and cultural mores.

This trip to Lebanon also gave me a richer understanding of why religions in this region have difficulty coexisting. The Muslim faith, in particular, demands much from its adherents in terms of public expressions of faith. Every night in Beirut, many people would gather in mosques for evening prayers and worship. However, the mosques are not content merely to have worship inside their sanctuary; they also use large amplifiers to carry the sounds of worship throughout the city. The "noisiness" of these practices makes religion very public in civil society. People do not engage in religion just within their own households, but do so in ways that intrude into the lives of all those around them. No one practices his or her beliefs quietly and keeps religion separate from others. The community prefers public expressions of religious sentiment, and this challenges the lives of others who hold alternative viewpoints.

What I witnessed in Beirut helped me understand the civic damage that can be done by intense religious conflicts and the difficulty of establishing a fully cooperative multisectarian society. In recent decades, Lebanon, along with its neighbors in Syria, Iraq, Jordan, and Egypt, have paid a steep price for societal conflict. Many of these countries have been torn apart by disputes between Sunnis and Shiites, or in some cases, Christians and Moslems. Mass violence has erupted and destroyed the possibility for political compromise and negotiation.

The Trip to Bahrain

A 2005 trip to Bahrain showed me other aspects of religious divisions. That Persian Gulf nation has a feudal leadership structure alongside modern skyscrapers and sophisticated technology. It is a small island country just off the coast of Saudi Arabia, and until 1986 no bridge linked the two countries. A causeway bridge built that year has been a boon to travel and trade between them.

Saudi Arabia is governed by a strict Islamic regime that allows no alcohol, music, or dancing—at least in public. However, many Saudis want these activities, so each weekend thousands of them drive over the causeway to Bahrain to partake of drinking, open socializing between the sexes, and entertainment such as Western movies. Local Bahrain residents are amused at the hypocrisy of their Saudi neighbors, who meekly accept social restrictions at home but are eager for more tolerant environs elsewhere.

Other aspects of Bahrain society are striking, including that high-tech innovators in a seemingly modern society appear to tolerate being ruled by an absolutist monarchy. Less surprising, but still disturbing, was how women are denied basic human rights such as voting and owning property. In this way the place is a throwback to the world of centuries ago. During my visit a local newspaper carried a column by a female writer condemning the decline of music and theater in Bahrain. She noted that local fundamentalists had complained about various performances being contrary to Islam. Rather than pushing back, local authorities simply shut down public performances.

One day, I had a perplexing encounter with a Muslim couple in the hotel elevator. My room was on the eleventh floor and I was going down to the lobby. I was in the corner of the elevator when it stopped at the tenth floor. At first, I didn't see anyone, but then a woman dressed in black walked into the elevator. Her face was completely veiled except for an inch-wide slit for her eyes. She was startled when she saw me, as was her husband, who was accompanying her. They whispered something in Arabic and then pressed the button for floor nine. They rode down one floor and got off.

As the door closed, I heard them push the button to call another elevator. Perhaps they had forgotten something and needed to go back up to their room. But judging from their clear discomfort at seeing me, it appeared they called another elevator because they didn't want to ride down to the lobby with a Western man. It was shocking that my presence as a middle-aged man made them uncomfortable, and the incident helped me understand how strongly religious sentiment can affect even routine aspects of people's daily lives.

Jewish Fundamentalists

On recent overseas flights, middle-aged American women have been shocked when Jewish Orthodox men assigned the seat next to them have refused to occupy the seat on religious grounds. According to news accounts, there have been a number of cases when Orthodox men asked female passengers to switch seats so they did not have to sit next to them. As explained by an Orthodox rabbi: "When I was still part of that community, and on the more conservative side, I would make every effort I could not to sit next to a woman on the plane, because of a fear that you might touch a woman by accident."[5]

Samuel Heilman, a Queens College sociology professor, says that this kind of segregation is important for certain parts of the Jewish community. "The ultra-Orthodox have increasingly seen gender separation as a kind of litmus test of Orthodoxy," he said. "There is an ongoing culture war between these people and the rest of the modern world, and because the modern world has increasingly sought to become gender neutral, that has added to the desire to say, 'We're not like that.'"[6]

Upset with this behavior, one 81-year-old Israeli woman named Renee Rabinowitz sued the El Al airline on grounds of gender discrimination. According to her, "The idea of having a Haredi [ultra-Orthodox] population is wonderful, as long as they don't tell me what to do." Continuing, she noted that "this is not personal. It is intellectual, ideological, and legal. I think to myself, here I am, an older woman, educated, I've been around the world, and some guy can decide that I shouldn't sit next to him. Why?"[7]

From this and other examples, it is clear how much religion complicates life in Israel. At the Wailing Wall in Jerusalem's Old City (the remaining part of the ancient Second Temple), there has been intense conflict over whether women should be allowed to pray with a Torah, the sacred Jewish scroll. A female protester complained that "the rabbinical authority doesn't want us there; they only want people who practice ultra-religious traditions to pray at the Wailing Wall."[8]

The dispute is emblematic of growing conflict between ultra-Orthodox and other elements within Israeli society. This division has provoked, or at least contributed to, sharp debates over such issues as whether ultra-Orthodox men have to serve in the military, the continued building of new settlements in the West Bank, transportation policy, laws affecting women, and foreign policy.[9]

With all these social and political tensions, Israelis argue with each other over whether their country can be Jewish and democratic at the same time.[10] That question reflects a toughening in attitudes against the nearly 1.8 million Arabs who live in Israel—most of them as citizens.[11] In a 2015 survey, for example, 48 percent of all Israeli Jews and 71 percent of Orthodox Jews in Israel agreed that "Arabs should be expelled or transferred from Israel" due to security concerns.[12] With Arabs representing 20 percent of the Israeli population, it is harder to reconcile democratic practices with policies emphasizing a Jewish identity.

One of many sources of tension within the country was a plan by the Israeli Defense Ministry to set up separate bus lines for Palestinians and Israelis traveling to the West Bank. For security reasons, some Jewish settlers had requested their own buses out of fear of Arab attacks. A legislator of the right-wing Jewish Home party told an Israeli newspaper that joint buses were "unreasonable" and complained that "the buses are filled with Arabs." Continuing, he said, "I wouldn't want my daughter to ride them" because of possible sexual harassment by Arab males.[13]

Others, though, fought this plan and said that it smacked of apartheid. Israeli President Reuven Rivlin complained that the pilot project "could have led to an unthinkable separation between bus lines for Jews and Arabs" and would "go against the very foundations of the state of Israel."[14] After public complaints, the project was shelved by the government.

There also are controversies in Israel over decisions to limit bus service on the Sabbath. The rationale is that "Orthodox Jews do not use motor vehicles on the Sabbath and holidays because of prohibitions on igniting fuel, creating sparks, and traveling beyond certain distances." Even though only one-fifth of Israeli Jews abide by these rules, religious officials cite them as among the decisions that make the country distinctive. "Imagine if there was public transportation on the streets like on weekdays. We would not know it is Shabbat in Israel," explained Rabbi Aryeh Stern of Jerusalem.[15]

Opponents have disputed this emphasis, however. "The religion is one aspect of Jewish culture, but it's not the only one. You can be a good Frenchman but not love baguettes or croissants; you can be a good Jewish citizen of the Jewish state but not take part of the religion," noted Jerusalem City Council representative Laura Wharton.[16]

A shift toward more restrictive dress codes has sparked a backlash among some Israeli school girls. Teachers and principals in strict Haredi religious schools that reject secular life have enforced government decisions to ban girls from wearing shorts to school while boys are allowed to do so. Under the new dictate, girls who wore shorts have been suspended from school and "blocked from taking important exams, having cell phones confiscated, and having their parents called in for their disciplinary infractions." According to press reports, certain school officials "accept the notion that rape and sexual harassment are linked to what a woman wears" and "the boys look" when girls wear shorts.[17] That led education officials to prevent girls from wearing shorts to school even when the temperatures are very high.

One school girl who was among those protesting this crackdown explained her rationale: "They educate girls to be ashamed of their bodies and to think that shorts are an invitation to rape. Girls don't have to feel bad about themselves because the administration is afraid of sexual harassment."[18]

However, the education ministry defended its dress code policy. When asked about the student protests, a top government official said: "The ministry instructs students and educators to come to school properly attired. It should be noted that in every school's regulations, which are set in consultation with the pupils and parents, there is a reference to the mode of dress which is determined according to the school community."[19]

Religious tensions furthermore have complicated Israeli social policy and foreign affairs. The country has taken a lurch to the right due to the power of religious minorities in the current governing coalition. Under the country's fractured political system, small political groups exercise disproportionate power, and some of them have insisted on policy concessions that have contributed to the failure of peace talks with Palestinians and have strained relations with other countries, including the United States.[20]

Most right-of-center political parties, for example, want to expand housing development in the West Bank even though that infuriates the Palestinians who live there. The latter view new settlements as a deliberate attempt by Israel to occupy the West Bank permanently and destroy the possibility of a fully functional Palestinian state. Even if Israel actively supported the idea of a two-state solution, the presence of Jewish settlements all over the West Bank could make it more difficult to implement peace agreements through land swaps needed to disentangle the Israeli and Palestinian communities.

Some of the Jewish settlers describe themselves as "the tip of the spear that protects Israel."[21] Others proclaim their interest in "establishing a Jewish kingdom based on the laws of the Torah. Non-Jews are to be expelled, the Third Temple is to be built, and religious observance is to be enforced, initially in public spaces."[22]

A few hardline settlers have been charged by the Israeli government with belonging to an extremist group known as "the Revolt." According to authorities, members of this network have engaged in terrorist attacks on Palestinians, including violence that killed women and infants. The group's manifesto pledges to "seek the collapse of the state of Israel, with its democratic government and courts, and the creation of a Jewish kingdom to replace it based on religious law."[23]

Hardline religious views also complicate daily life for Israeli Jews. For example, decisions regarding certain family policies have been transferred from the justice ministry to courts supervised by the religious services ministry that follow ultra-Orthodox legal doctrines. In one case, a woman named Sara Murray discovered, following her divorce, that parental custodian rights were tilted strongly in favor of men. Much to her shock, she found that it was difficult for her to see her six children. She had to check in with religious social workers and was not allowed to meet her offspring when she wanted.[24]

In short, Israel is the site of extraordinary conflict within and across religious cultures. There is intense controversy within the country about the role of religion in politics and society. Just as other nations are experiencing their own kinds of conflict between secular and orthodox beliefs, Israel is seeking to reconcile the openness of a very successful modern society with the dictates of religious sentiments rooted in centuries-old traditions. How those tensions play out will have tremendous consequences, not only for the country's domestic policies but also for Israel's standing in the global community of nations.

Islamic Fundamentalists

The radicalization of some Muslims plus the age-old conflict between Sunnis and Shiites, based on historical grievances, differing interpretations of religious texts, and deep cultural and socioeconomic differences, are major aspects of contemporary tension in the Middle East. But there also are complications when fundamentalists in each community take actions to oppose modernity and secularization, both within the region and in the West as well. Many of these individuals claim that Western culture corrupts women and young people and encourages immoral behavior.

When it was in power in Afghanistan during the 1990s, the Taliban banned television and Western music in some provinces, citing its corrupting impact. Militants in Logar province went to mosques and told people to quit watching television. "They threatened the people that 'if you do not give up watching television, you will face violence,'" said one local individual. The rationale was that "TV networks were showing programs that were 'un-Islamic and anti-Afghan culture.'"[25]

Using the same logic, Taliban fighters have burned girls' schools on grounds that women should not be educated. They also have demanded that shop owners stop selling music cassettes. When they were in charge of the Afghanistan government, Taliban militia would burn music tapes and beat drivers who listened to music cassettes in their cars. Some individuals claim that "Afghanistan is an Islamic country, and does not accept the foreign culture. These [music] shops have destroyed the lives of the youth and persuade them toward immoral crimes."[26]

The recent rise of the Islamic State of Iraq and al-Sham (ISIS) has drawn new attention to the methods of Islamic extremists.[27] Its forces have seized large parts of Iraq and Syria and imposed strict religious rules on local inhabitants. Those who do not accept their beliefs have been beheaded or shot. ISIS militants refer to opponents as the "moderns," meaning people who accept modernity and secularization.[28] They see themselves as supporting sacred values over corrupt and depraved Western norms.

Central to the ISIS belief is support for strict interpretations of religious texts. According to writer Graeme Wood, who has undertaken a detailed study of ISIS attitudes and behaviors, adherents "cannot waver from governing precepts that were embedded in Islam by the Prophet Muhammad and his earliest followers. They often speak in codes and allusions that sound odd or old-fashioned to non-Muslims, but refer to specific traditions and texts of early Islam."[29]

Some ISIS leaders have used these moral codes to justify sexual slavery of non-Islamic women. Believers of the Yazidi religion, a minority, for example, have been the victims of ISIS fighters who kidnapped thousands of girls and women and turned them into slaves. One 12-year-old girl who was assaulted said that her captor "told me that according to Islam he is allowed to rape an unbeliever. He said that by raping me, he is drawing closer to God."[30]

Journalist Anna Erelle interviewed jihadists regarding their longer-term views and ambitions. She says that a typical response includes the following sentiments: "The Islamic State will wage war on the United States and force its people to submit to God's will. Then we'll abolish all borders, and the earth will be one Islamic State under Sharia law."[31] ISIS fighter

Abu Bilel al-Firanzi justified these views by proclaiming that "being religious means imposing your values."[32]

An ISIS manual seized during a U.S. Special Forces raid revealed that the ISIS "caliphate" had organized structures for implementing its objectives. For example, the document outlined "departments to oversee the handling of war spoils including slaves, antiquities, and oil holdings." The manual, according to a U.S. government envoy, showed ISIS's "methods of subjugating people under their control."[33]

Studies of women who join ISIS find a variety of motivations linked to the desire for community. Researchers at King's College in London have studied 550 women from Western societies who joined the terrorist organization. "Much has been made of romantic notions in motivating people to go, but we know that reality is very different," said writer Melanie Smith, whose report noted that women are moved by "a sense of isolation [in the West], a feeling that the international Muslim community is under threat, and a promise of sisterhood, which was especially important for teenage girls."[34] The reality of the role of women under ISIS is harsh by Western standards. Along with other Islamic traditionalists, ISIS does not recognize that women have equal rights, deserve to be educated, should be able to buy and sell property, or have the right to participate in the political process.[35] Rather, they should respect the rights of their parents and husbands and shield themselves from the modern world. In its most extreme form, that means they should be accompanied by a male relative whenever they leave the home, should not be allowed to drive or participate in public life, and must cover themselves up to prevent having any part of their bodies seen by men who are not related.[36]

In Syria and Iraq, it is estimated that at least 20,000 foreign fighters have joined ISIS, which is about half of the group's overall military. ISIS fighters have come from ninety nations, including 4,000 from Western countries.[37] Experts who study these soldiers say that beheading adversaries or burning opponents alive is part of *qisas*, the "principle of equal retaliation under Islamic law. If someone is killed, you can kill the perpetrator. You can choose the means."[38] This sort of behavior is not seen as barbaric or unjust but as a justified response to Western insults, including the U.S. bombing of innocent civilians in Islamic communities. If Americans use unmanned drones to attack villages and kill women and children, ISIS fighters believe their response is defensible.

When ISIS moves into a town, it uses summary executions to intimidate the locals. Those residents who are not Muslim are given the option of converting to Islam or paying a fine for the privilege of practicing their own religion. Local women have been kidnapped and made into "brides" for Islamic fighters.[39] In any town, the group seeks to redirect anger against corrupt officials in Damascus or Baghdad. Women are told to wear "black, flowing chadors," and people are not allowed to smoke in public, only in their homes. Its fighters "smash statues 'worshiped by infidels in the past.'"[40]

With its control of territory comes the ability to levy taxes, fines, and tolls—and, in the case of Iraq, control revenue from oil sales. It is estimated that ISIS earns around $1 billion annually from people and businesses that operate within its self-proclaimed caliphate.[41] That large amount of money helps it to recruit fighters, finance suicide bombers, smuggle oil, and purchase armaments.

Christian Fundamentalists

The Middle East is not the only place experiencing conflict over religious beliefs. Although not as violent as Islamic conflicts or as intense as Israeli debates, a serious tug of war rages in the United States over the teaching of evolution in schools. Scientists report irrefutable proof that the Earth is 4.5 billion years old and that life evolved over hundreds of millions of years. Single-celled organisms changed into multi-celled forms, and these entities developed through complex pathways into invertebrates, insects, dinosaurs, mammals, fish, birds, and eventually human life itself.[42] There is abundant fossil evidence documenting the course of evolution.

Yet millions of Americans do not accept the vast weight of scientific evidence. They believe evolution is a false concept and that a relatively recent idea called "creationism" represents a more valid explanation of how the universe developed. According to that perspective, life came about because a superpowerful God formed the Sun, Earth, the rest of the Solar System, and everything else in the heavens. As laid out in Genesis, the Earth was created by God in a short period of time and humans were a divine inspiration, not the by-product of evolutionary change. Advocates of so-called "intelligent-design" play down geological and biological history in favor of divine providence. Life, they argue, developed because God willed it so. It was not a random outcome based on biological fitness and environmental adaptation.

Gallup surveys regularly show that around 40 percent of Americans prefer a creationism viewpoint over evolutionary explanations. Despite evidence of fossils, dinosaurs, and physical artifacts from millions of years ago, devout believers insist God created people in their present form within the last 10,000 years. These public opinion numbers have been consistent over the past thirty years.[43] It doesn't matter what is in the news or what kinds of scientific discoveries might have taken place—a substantial number of Americans accept only the biblical version of how the world in general, and humans in particular, came to be.

As a result of these beliefs, for decades schools around the country have been the scene of pitched battles about the proper curriculum. Secularists insist that schools follow scientific evidence and teach evolutionary perspectives. Many fundamentalists, however, claim evolution merely is a possible theory with no greater credibility than creationism, and that intelligent design frameworks deserve equal weight in science teaching within public school classrooms. Some places teach evolution and intelligent design as competing theories, which has the effect of making the nonscientific view just as credible as the one based on science.

The nation also faces serious fights over the validity of climate change. Nearly all scientists accept the factual evidence showing that the Earth's atmosphere is warming and the consequences will include rising oceans due to higher temperatures and the melting of ice sheets. Scientists have documented extensive evidence that the use of fossil fuels and hydrocarbons is a major contributor to these trends and that humans need to take major measures to prevent long-term planetary destruction.

Despite the hard evidence, many Americans do not accept these conclusions. They are skeptical of climate claims and argue that it is premature to take draconian measures when the evidence, in their view, is inconclusive. Gallup polling data show that 25 percent of Americans "are not worried about global warming much or at all" and that only 39 percent "attribute global warming to human actions."[44] So-called climate skeptics are suspicious of the scientific establishment and feel that natural causes of warming—if, indeed warming is taking place—are more important than human-related factors.

These disputes over evolution and climate change are of much more than academic importance and, in fact, are deeply relevant to U.S. domestic politics and public policy. The percentage of Americans with Christian fundamentalist beliefs remains significant and affects the politics of many communities (see figure 5-1). According to Gallup polls, about one-third of Americans think the Bible is the actual word of God.[45]

Fundamentalist Christians are a potent political force in the United States, especially within the Republican Party and in key Southern and Midwestern states. They exercise power disproportionate to their numbers because of their ability to sway elections in many states and localities.

Figure 5-2 presents the percentage of ordinary Americans who, since 1992, have called themselves "evangelical" or "born-again" Christians. For most of this time period, the number has been in the low to mid-40s.[46] The exact count ebbs and flows, depending on what is in the news and what issues occupy people's attention. But for the last two decades, it is clear that a substantial number of Americans identify themselves with evangelical Christianity. They support fundamental values and bring a religion-based moralistic perspective to bear on political and policy issues. They turn out to vote in large numbers and attract major political and other leaders to their public events.

The fact that so many Americans consider themselves as evangelical or fundamentalist is a major factor in contemporary elections, politics, and public policy. Those with strong religious beliefs tend to take starkly different positions on many issues from those with less dogmatic or even secular points of

FIGURE 5-1. *Bible as Actual Word of God*

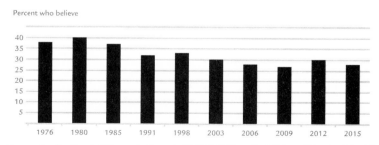

Percent who believe

Source: Lydia Saad, "Three in Four in U.S. Still See the Bible as Word of God," Gallup Poll, June 4, 2014.

FIGURE 5-2. *Evangelical Christians, 1992–2013*

Percent who believe

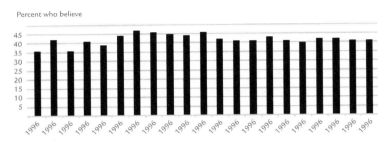

Source: Gallup Poll, "Religion," undated.

view. The moralistic tenor of civic dialogue complicates the solving of problems and contributes to the sharp polarization seen during recent years.

Many politicians go out of their way to cultivate religious voters. Early in the primary season for the 2016 elections, for example, Republican presidential candidate Rick Perry told an Iowa church audience that "I was going to spend the rest of my life doing God's work." Carly Fiorina, another GOP contender, explained to church-goers that "it was my husband Frank's and my personal relationship with Jesus Christ that saved us from a desperate sadness."[47]

Religion also affects how leaders define security issues. In his first presidential campaign ad called "A Civilizational Struggle," Republican Senator Marco Rubio described the current world situation as an epic morality tale involving attacks on Western society by radical Islam. Recalling the December 2015 terrorist attacks in Paris, Rubio's ad told potential voters: "This is a civilizational struggle between the values of freedom and liberty, and radical Islamic terror. What happened in Paris could happen here. There is no middle ground. These aren't disgruntled or disempowered people. These are radical terrorists who want to kill us, because we let women drive, because we let girls go to school."[48]

Apocalyptic Thinking

The sharp conflicts over science, religion, and modernity in many nations is emblematic of a world undergoing mega-change. As noted earlier, people with strongly held beliefs are among the forces that have increased the intensity of current disputes over politics, society, and religion. Because they tend to view compromise as surrender to immorality, voters with dogmatic opinions have made it difficult for leaders to negotiate over foreign and domestic policy. When individuals are certain that they have the truth—and that people who believe differently are not just wrong but possibly even evil—it is hard for them to tolerate other perspectives or agree to solutions that ask them to sacrifice important values.

Religious zealotry has always been with us but is particularly challenging in today's world because of the speed of global communication and the interactions among foreign and domestic policies. Extremism in one country sometimes generates extreme reactions elsewhere. When people in the West see ISIS beheading Christians and others, it leads to strong responses and calls for tough action to stop such heinous acts. The interactive nature of conflict can set off cycles of violence in which each action justifies the next reaction. Once set in motion, it is hard to stop these escalations.

In some places, clear strands of apocalyptic thinking actually encourage doomsday scenarios. Religious extremists see a coming megabattle between good (that is, themselves and those of like minds) and evil (everyone else). This expectation increases the odds of self-fulfilling actions that raise the intensity of conflict. In the biblical book of Revelation, for example, the writer John of Patmos forecasts a global battle between God and Satan culminating in Armageddon and the second coming of Jesus Christ.[49] He noted that in the lead-up to this gigantic fight, there will be unusual weather events such as volcanoes, earthquakes, and floods, along with dramatic geopolitical activities such as the rebuilding of a new temple in Jerusalem. To many believers, the apparent arrival of some of these things—climate change, for example—signals the end of the world and the need to prepare for the ultimate battle.[50]

Among other things, Christian fundamentalists cite these religious texts to justify their strong support of the state of Israel, and why the United States should as well. Since Jerusalem represents the spot where Jesus ascended to heaven more than 2,000 years ago, it also is the place where they think he will return to slay all nonbelievers and escort "the chosen" to eternal life in heaven.

In a similar vein, Islamic fundamentalists have a parallel view of religious destiny based on their reading of the Koran. In that view Allah and the Prophet Mohammad will save them and destroy all the infidels (nonbelievers) in an upcoming battle between good and evil. According to Brookings scholar William McCants, "The U.S. invasion of Iraq and the stupendous violence that followed dramatically increased the Sunni public's appetite for apocalyptic explanations of a world turned upside down. A spate of bestsellers put the United States at the center of the End-Times drama, a new 'Rome' careering throughout the region in a murderous stampede."[51] Other writers have echoed this concern, claiming that ISIS has an "overriding, apocalyptic mission: to lure the world's unbelievers into Syria for a final, Armageddon-like battle."[52]

Muslims with this apocalyptic vision condemn Israel for taking land and controlling the Temple Mount and its sacred Dome of the Rock and al-Aqsa Mosque, one of the most holy Islamic sites because it was from here that Mohammad rose to the "Divine Presence" on a winged horse. The Dome of the Rock celebrates this miraculous journey, central to Islam. Some Muslims have welcomed the introduction of Western troops in the Middle East because this enables them to prepare for battle and attracts adherents to their particular side. They believe Western nations are engaging in a war against Islam, and a climactic battle will save them from their current oppression.[53]

The Old City in Jerusalem is sacred in Judaism because of the Western Wall (or Wailing Wall), the only surviving part of the Second Jewish Temple that was burned by Romans in 70 A.D. For Jews, this place is called Mount Moriah (also known as Mount Zion) and it is the destination where they come to pray. Even though this would be extremely provocative to Muslims, some ultra-Orthodox believers hope some day to build a Third Temple on this site and restore the glory of their ancient faith.

Hence, there are apocalyptic strands in three of the world's monotheistic religions that complicate peace making and lead to dangerous domestic and foreign policy viewpoints. Religion historian Elaine Pagels notes that apocalyptic predictions have been around for centuries.[54] When people are under great stress and been severely oppressed, they often resort to predictions of doom and demise. It is only human under dire conditions to long for the end and hope for a heaven that brings peace and serenity to the true believers.

The risk today is that these apocalyptic visions collide in dangerous ways in the Middle East and elsewhere. Fundamentalists see rewards from taking extreme actions that will lead to the end of time and eternal salvation. There is no justification for compromise with those of opposing views. They see these conflicts as representing the will of God and fulfilling their historic destiny. For them, this cataclysmic confrontation will bring great glory, honor, and eternal salvation. Such extremist views antagonize other people and intensify international conflict.

CHAPTER SIX

The Challenges of Megachange

Megachange presents both risks and opportunities. During transformative periods, chaos and turbulence are quite likely. Large-scale shifts catch individuals off guard, creating tension and anxiety. People wonder how something not anticipated could happen and what it means for them personally. Since these developments often appear unexpectedly, there is little time to adjust, and it is difficult for policymakers to deal with the public anxiety and uncertainty that is unleashed by megachange.

But major transformation also presents some opportunities. The forces that destabilize modern life create possibilities to shift paradigms, alter assumptions, and forge new realities. It takes imagination and creativity to ponder new options, but shifting terrains makes it possible to develop fresh perspectives and novel strategies for moving forward.

In this chapter, I discuss the challenges of megachange for individuals, society, and governance. I show how large-scale change has upended people's comfort levels, led to massive population relocations, and created major governance problems. Currently, there is a mismatch between slow, deliberative political institutions and global change that is fast and widespread. Leaders need to improve governance processes so they can more quickly develop policies that help people deal with the personal and societal difficulties arising from megachange. If officials are not able to improve the way they handle large-scale transformation, societal progress could be reversed and current scientific and cultural gains diminished. Those far-reaching prospects demonstrate the importance of dealing with the aftermath of megachange.

The Challenge for Individuals

Dramatic shifts present many challenges for people at the personal level. Change, especially when it seems sudden or inexplicable, can cause stress, anxiety, and a sense of unrootedness. People feel de-anchored from forces that once provided stability to their lives. They worry about chaotic conditions and do not understand why things have shifted, forcing them out of their comfort zone.

This is one of the reasons why political and religious polarization has taken hold in many societies. When people feel adrift, they sometimes seek solace in religious or political doctrines that seem to provide clear-cut answers to uncertain situations. Having ready-made answers to complex problems helps to simplify the world and gives comfort to those coping with confusing circumstances. That is apparent for those with varying ideologies who dislike particular kinds of change, as well as more extreme radicals who want to take the world back several centuries due to their hatred of modern-day secularism.

If major change is inherently difficult for most people to accept, absolute chaos—the upending of societal norms as a result of war, economic collapse, or natural disasters—generates an even more serious backlash. When political earthquakes take place, they are hard to fathom and often produce overreactions by political leaders who feel they must respond to perceived threats. Anxiety and anger lead those afflicted by chaos to demand action to ensure their personal safety. The bad feelings generated by large-scale change produce calls for greater security, law and order, or actions designed to protect people from the fallout. Jingoistic rhetoric makes many people feel good even while it inflames tensions with adversaries and generates a new round of extremism.

As pointed out in earlier chapters, change in one direction can generate strong passions from the other side. Unintentionally, some actions that appear defensive to one side may come across as offensive to the other side. It is easy for escalations to compound problems and make it even more difficult to defuse tensions.

In these types of situations, global leaders have to be careful to avoid scenarios in which change takes place so rapidly that it destabilizes people's personal comfort zones. If alterations make people feel worse about their own futures, it will stimulate desires to return to familiar orthodoxies or encourage people to turn toward authoritarian leaders. There are historical antecedents for these fears. During the Great Depression of the 1930s, when economic disruptions traumatized millions of people, citizens in several countries turned to dictators as a way to deal with chaos and disorder. In Germany, Adolf Hitler took advantage of deep economic stress to blame scapegoats, notably Jews and communists.[1] Benito Mussolini promised Italians that he would take control of chaotic conditions in that country so that "the trains ran on time."[2]

This is the danger we face again today—that economic and social stress arising from tremendous change will stoke extremism, including a desire for order to deal with the resulting chaos. For example, middle-class workers in much of the developed world face stagnating incomes, limited social mobility, and high levels of inequality.[3] All these forces put them under great stress and encourage some of them to turn to demagogues or ultra-nationalists promising easy solutions.

During periods of tremendous uncertainty, some people blame modernity and secularization for the anxiety they feel. In today's world, they question the value of globalization and the free flow of goods and services. They wonder whether capitalism and democracy serve their interests. For certain individuals, alienation and resentment lead them to want to turn back the clock to earlier times and adhere to what they consider tried-and-true philosophies for coping with the world. Longing for protection and traditional cultural values is a common response when people face high stress and experience anxiety.

The Challenge for Society

There also are dramatic social consequences of megachange. Big forces affect societies, organizations, and social interactions. Disruptions influence not only how people feel and act, but the way they live and organize themselves with their friends and neighbors.

The clearest evidence comes from the massive population shifts that have grabbed the world's attention in recent years. Today, there are population migrations, resettlements, refugees from civil war and social conflict, and public displacements on a grand scale. In some societies, extreme poverty and social dislocation lead to trafficking in human beings across national borders.

As of late 2015, according to the United Nations refugee agency, nearly 60 million people had been displaced from their homes in Africa, the Middle East, Asia, and Latin America.[4] Syria's civil war is perhaps the best-known and most urgent current refugee situation. The civil war has forced about half of the country's 22 million people out of their homes, most of them having fled to other parts of the country. Another 4 million Syrians have sought refuge in Turkey, Lebanon, Jordan, or Europe.[5] Afghanistan also has undergone the latest of a series of refugee crises with some 2.6 million people having fled to neighboring countries, or as far away as Europe, to escape continuing conflict.

Virtually every continent has seen large changes in where people live and work. For example, African civil wars since the late 1990s, especially in the Great Lakes region and the Horn of Africa, have created several waves of refugees and internally displaced people (those who stay in their own countries after fleeing their homes). Most of them have fled to neighboring countries, but an increasing number have migrated north in hopes of making it to Europe. They endure great deprivation and even death while on the move, including an untold number who drown while trying to cross the Mediterranean Sea.

Many poor migrants spend their entire life savings, at times thousands of dollars, to escape shocking violence at home for hope of better lives in unknown destinations abroad. Their home countries have been torn apart by military invasion, ethnic conflict, or civil strife. They often are forced to flee their hometowns with little more than what they can carry on their backs. Sometimes, they must walk hundreds of miles in order to save themselves and their families.

Mass migrations can lead to a backlash against those who have been forced to move or have left their homelands voluntarily in search of better lives. For example, many European nations and places such as Australia have reacted quite negatively to the flood of Syrian and other refugees who have appeared at their borders. To deal with this human tide, some have adopted a "containment" strategy based on building fences to prevent refugees crossing from neighboring countries. Hungary has built "a 109-mile fence to keep out those hoping to enter the

European Union from Serbia." In addition, Bulgaria wants to extend a current fence with Turkey by another 80 miles to keep migrants out.[6] In this and other ways, the backlash from the 2015 refugee crisis threatened to upend the conventional politics of several countries. Far-right, anti-immigrant political parties have gained renewed traction across much of Europe, including in Austria, Denmark, France, Germany, the Netherlands, and Norway. In 2016 a far-right candidate in Austria came very close to winning the presidency (a symbolically important, though largely figurehead office) based in part on unease about refugees.

The United States has accepted very few refugees from Syria and other recent conflict zones, but some politicians have taken advantage of voter angst about terrorism and economic distress. In his campaign for the Republican presidential nomination, Donald Trump, for example, proposed building a "wall" to protect the United States from immigrants arriving from Mexico, Central America, and South America. There already is a fence along portions of the border with Mexico, but Trump gained considerable attention and political support by demanding more substantial barriers and even the expulsion of the some 11 million "illegal" (officially "undocumented") Mexicans now in the United States.

Given the great danger posed by Trump-like rhetoric, political authorities must develop more rational means to deal with massive population shifts and the human traumas they represent. Leaders should restructure development activities to alleviate poverty and the causes of civil conflict, and thus help people in troubled lands move into productive lives. Widespread resettlement has destabilized the world and detached tens of millions of people from their normal social, economic, and political communities. If we don't improve this reality, many nations will have a new permanent underclass composed of people with little future. That is tragic for those directly affected and detrimental for society in general. Deprivation and lack of hope beget crime and violence, which exacerbates social tensions.

In this state of affairs, terrorism and destructive violence will become the new normal. This already is the case in several parts of the developing world; extremism and organized violence also are becoming more common in the developed world. When various sides justify extremist tactics as payback for past grievances, it is difficult to resolve conflict through peaceful solutions. Instead, armed combatants seek mastery over their adversaries and have few incentives to accept peaceful, negotiated solutions.

The Challenge for Governance

Improving governance represents one of the greatest challenges of our time. In much of the developing world, government institutions either are weak and ineffective or rigid and authoritarian. Most Western democracies, by contrast, have institutions that work slowly through deliberative political processes—and thus are not very adept at dealing with fast change. Democratic practices were designed for an agricultural era when change was incremental and small-scale.

As a result, many civic processes around the world are ill-equipped to deal with fast-paced megachanges. Dramatic advances in world events, genetics, robotics, and artificial intelligence, for example, outpace our ability to understand their consequences. Even though our communications and technologies are twenty-first century, the formal governance structures that must deal with changes were designed at least one or two centuries ago.

The consequence is a mismatch between domestic governance and global change. We need institutions and processes that make faster decisions and put national governments in a stronger position to address large-scale transformation. This means updating our information-gathering and analysis capabilities and figuring out better ways to incorporate up-to-the-minute material into real-time decisionmaking. It is vital to upgrade our institutions and processes so that leaders can react quickly to changing realities.

Too often, leaders get vital information days, weeks, or even months after they have to make decisions. The result is choices that are not well informed or based on obsolete data. Depending on the issue at hand, that result can be catastrophic for the country. Especially in a situation posing grand challenges and requiring big decisions, there must be a closer connection between on-the-ground realities and effective decisionmaking. If leaders don't have reliable information, their choices could very well make a bad situation even worse.

In addition, many societies have a fundamental institutional problem in which small or narrow-focus factions exercise disproportionate influence—often due to election rules. For example, in parliamentary systems with very low thresholds for legislative representation, tiny parties with extreme agendas can become major power-brokers because larger parties need them to form ruling coalitions. The extreme party can therefore demand and get major concessions that force public policy into an extreme direction.

This has happened in recent Israeli elections. The ruling conservative Likud party has formed coalitions with extreme religious and nationalist parties, with dramatic consequences for domestic and foreign policies. Small groups have insisted on expansion of West Bank settlements and religious rules that have increased conflict within the country and undermined Israel's standing around the world. This is an example of how the technicalities of political processes can exacerbate conflict and make problem resolution much more difficult.

There have been similar dynamics in the United States, where special interest groups exercise disproportionate power because of their real or imagined political influence. The National Rifle Association (NRA) is a prominent illustration of this problem. Guns continue to be easy to purchase in most states and, without federal restrictions on the kinds of guns that can be purchased, are easily moved from state-to-state. Despite numerous mass killings, the NRA blocks any efforts, at the state or national levels, to outlaw assault weapons, to ban the sale of high-cartridge munitions, or to require more detailed background checks, including for people with a history of violence or mental health problems. The group's leaders argue that gun laws violate the Constitution and that people need more guns, rather than fewer of them—including high-powered weapons intended for military use—to defend themselves. Given the NRA's adamant opposition, it has been difficult, and usually impossible, to enact reasonable gun laws that protect society as a whole. The NRA and other organized groups prevent the United States from doing what most Western societies have done, which is use gun access laws to reduce violence in the society.

Finding ways to build consensus is essential during an era of major transformation. If change makes people nervous and political rules empower small groups with extreme agendas, the result can be a recipe for disaster in policymaking and governance. The combination of extremism and extensive change makes it doubly hard for societies to develop viable compromises that are both effective and acceptable to broad segments of society.

Weakening Political Extremism

One of the difficulties made complicated by today's mega-changes and faced by leaders is to solve the puzzle of extremism and improve governance. The tidal wave of change has uprooted people and created enormous difficulties because there is a common human tendency to resist accepting people from different backgrounds, especially those with starkly different worldviews.

In his book *The Big Sort*, journalist Bill Bishop argues that certain contemporary trends aggravate this problem. For example, people have divided themselves into a variety of separate and isolated contexts.[7] This is the case, for example, in housing, education, and cultural activities. Individuals have preferred to surround themselves with those having like-minded viewpoints and shun information that does not support their own prejudices. This widespread sorting has made it nearly impossible for modern societies to retain the sense of community that once bound people together. When different communities have competing values, backgrounds, and alternative points of view, it can be challenging for them to negotiate with each other and resolve conflicts. The clash of fundamental values increases polarization and misunderstanding, encourages extremism, and undermines trust in the underlying social and political fabric.

While many aspects of modern times make it difficult for people to come together, one of the major disruptors has been digital technology and instantaneous communications. In areas from computers and microprocessors to smartphones and remote sensors, technology has remade entire fields and altered how people interact with each other and conduct business.[8]

Scientific advances also have sped the rate of change. Biomedical gains in understanding of genetics, neuroscience, and cloning raise ethical questions that complicate problem solving. When people see scientists appearing to play God by altering life in fundamental ways, even in ways that save lives, it challenges their belief systems and sense of ethics. Modern practices, from animal cloning to genetic modification of food and in vitro fertilization, can generate considerable anxiety and lead to a backlash against scientific practices.

The broad scale of political, social, and economic change has unnerved people and led some to fear modernity and secularization.[9] In developing nations, for example, it is difficult to persuade some people to accept modern ideas and practices because they see few economic or social benefits from globalization and secularization. They worry that a rush into the future is disrupting their communities and failing to respect traditional ways of thinking.

Disruptions can be problematic when they destabilize common patterns of communications and commerce and established patterns of interaction. Many people have lost touch with others in society or had jobs that were eliminated. They see the downside of economic or cultural change, and this makes them susceptible to extremist ideologies. As Muslim writer Laila Lalami notes, it becomes difficult to be a moderate in the face of extremist behavior by other people.[10]

To resolve social and political tensions, people must learn to share benefits more broadly. As long as extreme elements dominate politics and winners benefit disproportionately, governance will serve narrow constituencies, and others will feel left out of the benefits. In this situation, cynicism prevails, making it even harder for society to deal with megachange.[11] Leaders have to realign contemporary processes to serve all of their constituencies and match the speed and scale of twenty-first-century transformations.

One necessary element is moving toward broader political participation. In the United States, low voter turnout has encouraged extremist politics and political polarization. When only 55 to 60 percent of eligible voters cast ballots in presidential races, around 40 percent vote in off-year congressional contests, and 10 to 20 percent participate in local elections, politicians have incentives to play to the base, take extreme positions, and eschew bargaining and negotiation as signs of a lack of political principle. Rather than focusing on the middle and seeking compromise, too often they take nonnegotiable stances and refuse to acknowledge the possible validity of alternative viewpoints. The result is a system that is gridlocked and plagued by a winner-take-all mentality.

Universal voting offers the potential to disrupt these negative incentives.[12] More than two dozen countries, such as Australia and Belgium, require citizens to vote and, in some cases, require non-voters to pay a small civil fine.[13] Some of these countries have electoral participation that is well over 90 percent. This type of reform could fundamentally alter the electoral incentives facing leaders, creating the possibility for more broad-based appeals and less political extremism. According to Brookings Institution scholars William Galston and E. J. Dionne: "Intense partisans are more likely to participate in lower-turnout elections while those who are less ideologically committed and less fervent about specific issues are more likely to stay home."[14] Having a universal voting requirement offers the potential to change the current electoral dynamic.

Another improvement would come from thinking about ways to depolarize traditional and social media. Many political leaders face difficult situations because the modern information environment is intense and much of what is reported as "news" is based on opinions rather than facts. Cable television, in particular, too often fails to separate the serious from the trivial, and social media encourages extreme rhetoric. Ordinary citizens often have trouble distinguishing facts from strongly held opinions. Much of the news media also resemble echo chambers where like-minded people get news from sources that reinforce existing (and sometimes extreme) beliefs.[15]

Columnist Anne Applebaum bemoans "the disappearance of facts and the growth of Internet fantasy." She worries that "lies are acclaimed" and statistics are "invented" by "fake websites and dubious organizations."[16] Widespread suspicions of the mainstream news media mean no one has across-the-board credibility to report the news or decry false narratives. What is needed is news coverage that alters that dynamic and breaks down the polarization and extremism of contemporary discourse. Democracies cannot function without information systems that provide pertinent facts, nonpolarized commentary, and effective oversight of political leaders. Unless the general public demands improved media coverage and social media analysis, it will be impossible to stop political extremism and deceptive appeals.

The Reversibility of Progress

In recent decades scientific and technical advances have come at a pace unprecedented in human experience. Humans are exploring space, deciphering DNA, designing computers with enormous processing power—and even creating "artificial intelligence" capable of replicating what humans can do. With all of these activities, it sometimes seems that "progress" always is moving forward. Each new discovery adds to the foundation of public knowledge, and this is why we've come to expect these "quantum leaps" to always lead us forward, and never backward.

Yet when one looks at long-term history, change does not always advance forward or represent true progress. The Egyptians built the pyramids and revolutionized engineering. Operating several millennia ago, their engineers figured out how to transport great blocks of stone over long distances and use pulleys to lift these objects in the construction of towering buildings. In the process, they revolutionized science and math and gained a high level of knowledge.

The ancient Greeks also made tremendous advances in knowledge. Drawing on the insights of his forbearers, Euclid compiled many of the basic concepts of geometry in use today. This included the definition of a line and an understanding of angles. Pythagoras diagrammed the properties of triangles and determined how to compute the area of a circle. But during the Roman Empire foreign invaders burned the Old Alexandria library, and there was a startling loss of scientific knowledge from the Western world. After 500 A.D. a "Dark Ages" descended throughout Europe and the Mediterranean region, slowing the development of new knowledge and technology for nearly a millennium.

Not until the Renaissance was knowledge rekindled and science advanced again to new heights. Newton, Copernicus, and Galileo, among others, developed great insights into astronomy and dramatically altered our view of the universe. No longer would the Earth be seen as the center of the solar system but only as one planet revolving around the sun.[17] Religious leaders, however, fought these gains because they challenged assumptions based on readings of the Bible, but, with time, society was able to overcome those who wanted to preserve traditional beliefs and ways of doing things.

The post–Roman Empire period in Europe is not the only period when history has moved backward. The bidirectional nature of historic progress is revealed in the case of advances in math and science in the Islamic world. While Europe was mired in the Dark Ages, scholars in the Middle East achieved tremendous advances in learning. Innovators proposed the notion of zero, which helped them address mathematical issues. They furthermore made great strides in algebra to help them keep track of land boundaries. The astrolabe helped explorers accurately chart sunrises and sunsets.

Yet, today, many Arab countries have fallen far behind the West in scientific and mathematical knowledge. Almost-feudal political systems in most of the Middle East and North Africa have slowed innovation, and a religious orthodoxy regiments societies. Scientists in much of the region no longer press the boundaries of invention, and, with the exception of the energy sector, specifically oil, this has slowed economic growth.

Many observers look at advanced scientific societies today and conclude that leading nations in America, Europe, and East Asia are not likely to step backward. Most countries in these areas are advanced in terms of scientific knowledge, cultural tolerance, and cosmopolitanism—and they have prospered based on technological innovation that has sent men to the moon, explored the solar system, and launched space telescopes that can see back to the earliest days of the universe.

Yet even with these dramatic gains in knowledge, the United States now stands out as a place where there is a war on science. Many Americans don't believe in evolution and doubt the reality of global climate change. Some question the value of childhood vaccinations, despite clear evidence about their medical contributions.[18] The United States combines extraordinary advances in science with millions of people who doubt empirical evidence and believe that experts are frauds.

Advanced technology does not necessarily protect the notion of scientific progress. Internet evangelist Vint Cerf has warned about a "digital dark age" in which storage technologies change so much that knowledge gets lost. Rather than safeguarding information, rapid technological change can endanger knowledge preservation and lead to information retrogression because today's operating system does not understand yesterday's and might not communicate with tomorrow's.[19]

Political environments can change nearly as quickly as technology. As an example, much of Europe has been wracked with conflict over immigration and national identity. The post–World War II emphasis on tolerance and multiculturalism has given way to fears that the "French," "British," or "Norwegian" ways of life are being lost due to the influx of people who do not share native cultural values. There are significant social and political movements to close off borders, keeping out both people from other European countries and refugees fleeing war and oppression in distant lands. Writing 2,500 years ago, Greek philosopher Heraclitus pronounced that "a human cannot step into the same river twice in his or her lifetime, meaning that everything is bound to keep changing."[20] His view was that transformation is a given and people should anticipate rapid change.

Yet that insight often is lost in today's world. Unless we overcome presentism and recognize the high speed and magnitude of change, we will be unable to deal with its surprising character and unanticipated consequences. Opinion leaders need to recognize that dramatic shifts are occurring, even inevitable, and that the current era is less anchored and more unpredictable than they expect. Learning to navigate a world of extremism and megachange, without going backward, is a fundamental challenge of modern times.

CHAPTER 7

Navigating the Future

In many science fiction plots, "wormholes" connect galaxies and provide useful shortcuts for those seeking to navigate the universe. These galactic thoroughfares speed space-time transitions and help travelers deal with uncertainty along the route. Rather than struggling to handle the grand scale of the universe, fast lanes help people to cope with possible dangers along the journey.[1]

The fictional shortcuts raise the question of whether in real life there are analogous mechanisms that help humans deal with social, political, and economic transformations. In a world of megachange driven by religious conflict, ultra-nationalism, military aggression, economic turmoil, and technological advances, people need a means to deal with difficult interactions. Change often is tumultuous, chaotic, and non-linear, and it is not easy to determine how to respond to various disruptions.

In this chapter, I examine strategies for handling megachange. I argue that people need to broaden their horizons, find anchors that help them deal with large-scale transformations, and understand that small shifts can have tremendous ramifications. More broadly, societies need to emphasize moderation, rather than radical extremes, and end the winner-take-all mentality that elevates the stakes of great change. Until leaders figure out how to deal with the turbulence of societal alterations, there will continue to be chaos in domestic and global affairs.

Broadening Horizons

One important aspect of navigating current affairs is to understand the dramatic pace of contemporary change. Many people underestimate the possibilities of sudden and massive shifts and therefore are completely unprepared when something they didn't anticipate comes to pass. We see this all the time with weather events. People get used to certain meteorological patterns and are surprised by megastorms or extreme weather events. Hurricanes, tornadoes, droughts, or floods not only are devastating but can be especially shocking if unexpected.

Part of the problem is that many people's imaginations are hobbled by the recent past. Their set of possibilities includes only things that happened in a previous few years or decades. When an event takes place on a scale not seen in 100 years, they are amazed because it never happened during their lifetimes. Yet the only reason they are surprised is because of their own short time horizon. If they had a longer perspective, they would be less likely to be caught off-guard. They would understand that what is rare in a short time-frame can seem almost commonplace when considered during a lengthier perspective.

Looking at old maps can help people appreciate the possibilities of large-scale change. In examining historic depictions of the world, it is clear that maps provide a record of shifting social, economic, and political realities over a long period of time. Geopolitical boundaries move with considerable regularity across centuries. City names shift as do those of countries.[2]

Maps from the eighteenth and early nineteenth centuries are interesting because they reveal crucial things about that time. They emphasize rivers and waterways because those were the primary means of trade and commerce. By the twentieth century, though, rivers had given way in importance to railroads, highways, and airports. What people valued changed and maps had to present information in different ways. Rivers became less vital and highways more crucial to commerce and transportation.

Name shifts over time are not unusual. Cities get larger, or maybe even smaller, rural areas become urban, territory is taken over by different entities—all reflected in maps. When designations change, it generally is because something in society, politics, or identity has moved in a fundamental way.[3] What made a particular label relevant at one point in time gives way to a new reality.

Geopolitical considerations are a major reason for name shifts, as are changing economic or military fortunes. The modern city of Jakarta, Indonesia, for example, has undergone several alterations as various colonial powers overran the area. In the seventeenth and eighteenth centuries, the city was known as Batavia and was the headquarters of the Dutch East Indies Trading Company. Ships stopped there to pick up spices and supplies along their global excursions. But when the city was occupied by the Japanese during the mid-twentieth century, it became Jakarta.[4] The conquering power wanted its own name for the metropolitan area. It retains that name today even though Indonesia has been an independent nation for nearly seventy years.

The name of the body of water between Iran and Saudi Arabia depends greatly on geopolitical points of view. Iranians refer to it as the Persian Gulf, in honor of the ancient empire that controlled that territory; this also is the common designation in much of the West. Iran bans books that do not adhere to that terminology. However, in neighboring Saudi Arabia, geographers call it the Arabian Gulf, and countries on the Arabian Peninsula use that designation and insist their publications use that name. According to regional experts, the name dispute is "deeply emotional; it's not simply semantic."[5]

Perhaps the most striking example, though, has taken place elsewhere in the Middle East. As the historic crossroads of several civilizations, the area now known as Israel has gone through tumultuous shifts in political control over the millennia. In ancient times, one of the three components of Israel was known as Judea (the others being Samaria and the Galilee). But as the area was overrun by Egyptians, Greeks, Romans, Persians, Ottoman Turks, British, French, and Arabs, its name changed to Palestine and became just another foreign province for each conquering power. Each name reflected new geopolitical configurations and fresh national loyalties.

Geographic names and building designations have great meaning for people because of what they represent in terms of religion, economics, and politics. Each name means something completely different to the affected groups. It is not just the name change as much as the shift in the underlying identity and representation.

Today's globalized world has affected everyone's sense of time and distance. International trips require sometimes only a few hours' plane ride and cross thousands of miles. Passengers alight in localities where they often don't understand the language, the culture, or the political system, yet they are able to figure out how to navigate this new landscape, at least on the surface.

In a similar manner, realities that at first sight seem fixed turn out to be more fluid when viewed with a broader lens. Table 7-1 presents a revealing description of the risk of asteroids hitting the Earth based on size and frequency of occurrence. In looking at short time horizons, there is virtually no risk to planet Earth from relatively small stellar objects. Asteroids of sixteen feet in diameter enter Earth's atmosphere once every three years and produce a bright fireball in the sky but pose little risk to people or property.[6]

Yet when one lengthens the time horizon and considers larger objects, the risk profile changes dramatically. In 2013 a meteor measuring about sixty-five feet in diameter entered Earth's atmosphere and exploded about eighteen miles above Chelyabinsk, Russia. That detonation injured 1,500 people and damaged thousands of buildings, mostly from flying glass broken by the shock wave. It was the largest such force to hit the planet in nearly 100 years.[7]

According to astronomer David Eicher, Earth faces a major risk of mass extinctions once every 100 million years from space objects six miles in diameter or greater.[8] This is about the size of the object that hit the Earth 66 million years ago during the Cretaceous period and destroyed three-quarters of plant and animal species, including the dinosaurs.[9] That single asteroid changed the course of global history and paved the way

TABLE 7-1. *Asteroid Risk*

Asteroid size	Result	Frequency of occurrence
16 feet	Bright fireball	3 years
82 feet	Airburst event	200 years
164 feet	Local devastation	2,000 years
460 feet	Regional devastation	20,000 years
985 feet	Continental devastation	70,000 years
1,970 feet	Widespread devastation	200,000 years
0.6 mile	Global catastrophe	700,000 years
3 miles	Global catastrophe	30 million years
6 miles	Mass extinction	100 million years

Source: David Eicher, "Asteroid Day," Astronomy, July, 2015, p. 35.

for new species to arise. Eventually, the emergence of mammals led to the development of our own species, homo sapiens.

In looking at the grand scale of global history, it is readily apparent that we need to expand our time horizons. Judging the risk of certain events depends almost entirely on assumptions about time frames. Based on the time horizon and magnitude of the event imagined, there are systematically different probabilities of natural events such as hurricanes, typhoons, and asteroids to man-made occurrences such as world wars, economic recessions, and political revolution.

Expecting that laws, norms, national boundaries, or human behavior are going to change only in an incremental fashion is completely misleading. Both natural and human history are more relativistic and less constrained than we generally believe. We need to apply that insight to the worlds of politics, economics, and society.[10] People should not believe that low-probability events never will happen because they have not taken place in the last few decades. That is a failure of human imagination, and it blinds observers to the reality of the world's own history.

Finding Anchors

Interactions with people who are substantially different from oneself can pose many challenges, notably misunderstandings over fundamental values or an inability to grasp the motivations or intentions of people from different backgrounds or cultures. Throughout history, wars have begun over differences in religions, nationalities and race, politics, or economic imperatives. Encounters across civilizations usually have not gone well for the weaker side.

Due to globalization, migration, and improved transportation and communication, many people now encounter others from different backgrounds and cultures on a regular basis.

It no longer is uncommon in European or American cities, for example, to see women dressed in traditional hijabs, head scarves, or saris. Westerners, and Western culture, are as much a part of cities in Africa and Asia as well.

In a multicultural world, we need to figure out ways to overcome differences and understand how to deal constructively with those who don't share our basic beliefs. At times in the past, there was an inviolable faith in education and cultural exchange as ways to promote understanding—a belief that people developed a better understanding of others by bringing them all together. This also was a central pillar in the founding of the United Nations, for example.

Of course, it is harder for many people to accept that premise today given the frequency of regional wars, ethnic cleansing, and intercultural conflict. Cultural exchanges clearly are not effective in all situations. And, in some situations, more contact might even exacerbate conflict and tension, not promote more tolerance and better understanding. Moderation is not the only product of social, economic, or political experiences. Sometimes, extremism and intolerance arise from encounters that go awry.

The recent experience of Muslim immigrants in Europe demonstrates how difficult it is for new arrivals. Some first- and second-generation immigrants, in particular, have grown disenchanted with Western life and concluded that modern civilization is corrupt, unfair, and immoral. Blatant discrimination and the West's focus on consumerism and acceptance of permissive sex are regular complaints of many European Muslims.

It is not clear whether improved education remains the key to promoting international understanding. We have to figure out how to deal with other people and bridge cross-cultural divides without getting anxious, fearful, or angry. People do not have to believe the same things in order to get along day-to-day. They simply need to find things that anchor their existence, such as a home, a job, or a value system. Something that happens a lot, especially during a period of megachange, is misperception of another person's intentions. That creates tensions and increases the potential for conflict.

Understanding That Small Shifts Can Have Great Impact

Several examples of seemingly small changes in recent American elections have produced out-sized consequences. For example, some elections have been decided by very close margins, but the policy ramifications were enormous. Just because a campaign is close does not mean that its impact will be small or incremental in nature. Tight victories can provide the basis for large-scale policymaking.

Perhaps the most memorable example of this took place in 2000, with the highly contested race between Republican George W. Bush and Democrat Al Gore. Controversies over hanging chads in Florida and vote-counting procedures went all the way to the U. S. Supreme Court before being decided in a five-to-four vote in favor of Bush.[11] Despite the narrow court margin and the small difference in voting outcomes, that fateful decision gave all of Florida's Electoral College votes to Bush and therefore allowed him to win a 271 to 266 victory over Gore.

At the time, few observers anticipated the tremendous policy changes that would come out of that election. Bush, however, decided to govern as if he had won a landslide victory, adopting aggressively conservative policies on taxes, regulation, environmental protection, and other matters. Less than nine months after Bush took office, terrorist attacks in New York City and Washington, D.C., gave the president even more leverage to move the country significantly to the right. Bush proposed, and a compliant Congress passed, legislation that would transform a wide range of domestic and foreign policies.

The country would launch a "war on terror" that would systematically alter international affairs and domestic practices. The United States and its allies used the September 11 terrorist attacks as justification to invade and oust the governments of Afghanistan and Iraq; the resulting wars were still active, in varying ways, fifteen years later.

One result of Bush's wars was that many people in Islamic nations became fearful that the West was attacking Islam and embarking on a new "crusade" against its followers. Poorly chosen words used by some political leaders reinforced those concerns and helped inspire attacks against Westerners around the world. Luxury hotels and restaurants would be bombed and suicide attacks would become more frequent. Radical groups such as al Qaeda and ISIS would succeed in recruiting fighters from both the Middle East and the West.

In a time of megachange involving terrorism and global disorder, there are two very different risks. The first is the risk that people will underestimate change. It is easy to go into denial and ignore big trends that take place. People are surprised when large events happen that they had not anticipated. Rather than seeing incremental models as being the most likely, people need to anticipate and be open to nonlinear change and the chaotic policymaking that often results.

On the other hand is the very different risk of overreaction to widespread transformation. Global change can happen fast and create high levels of stress and anxiety. In that situation, it is possible to overreact and undertake rash actions that make bad problems even worse. Individuals and even entire countries can act in ways that aggravate tensions and increase misunderstanding.

The U.S. response to the 9/11 attacks falls within that latter category. In an effort to protect national security, President Bush launched two wars that unsettled global affairs and ultimately increased international conflict.[12] The U.S. invasions of two Islamic countries led many people in the Islamic world to see American policy as endangering them. Rather than decreasing global support for terrorism, U.S. military intervention gave radicals new ammunition for their argument that the West was out to destroy Islam—and that all weapons, including terrorism, were needed to counter that threat.

As always throughout history, this kind of misunderstanding presents grave threats to the world. If political leaders exaggerate threats or misperceive current dangers, they undertake actions that are not properly calibrated to existing realities. They go too far and inadvertently create a situation that leads to unnecessary conflict and provokes additional rounds of extremism and violence.

Ending Winner-Take-All

Megachange is especially problematic when conflict is conducted on a winner-take-all basis. As opposed to negotiated solutions where each side gets a little of what it wanted, today's conflicts elevate the stakes and intensity of disagreements. People fight to the finish, whether in civil wars and terrorism or the less violent pursuits of politics and international commerce. When they perceive the stakes to be really high, people will take excessive risk, engage in extreme actions, and cut ethical corners because they think the ends justify the means.

In the case of ISIS, its fighters believe that beheading opponents and other forms of brutality are reasonable because these actions represent a justified response to Western attacks against Islam, including U.S. use of drones to kill Islamic radicals in the region. ISIS leaders and followers appear to believe that striking out at the West will take them closer to their goal of creating an Islamic caliphate. When people have these kinds of lofty ambitions, it doesn't matter if they harm women and children, prolong the agony of adversaries, or engage in gruesome violence. The complaints about such practices are perceived as trivial compared to the scope of the goals that ISIS leaders have.

There are problematic dynamics in economics as well. A very small number of individuals around the world have amassed tremendous wealth. While some of them use their money to promote the common good, a number seem intent on resisting higher taxes or policies that help the less fortunate gain an education or start a business. They want to preserve their fortunes, even when this prevents others from getting ahead or having the money for basic necessities. These actions perpetuate an "us" versus "them" mentality and make it more difficult to resolve conflicts peacefully.

Combating the winner-take-all mentality that permeates many societies would help to reduce the stakes of conflict and weaken the intensity and polarization that afflicts contemporary politics. We need to figure out ways to de-escalate conflict and widen the number of winners. When people perceive conflict as a zero-sum game, it encourages extremism and immoderation. Moving politics to positive-sum outcomes would ease people's anxieties and increase incentives for bargaining and negotiation of differences. In the long run, this would take some of the intensity out of current conflict, reduce polarization, and make people more tolerant of political disagreements.

Deradicalizing Civil Society

In too many countries, extremism and zealotry abound in schools, religious institutions, advocacy organizations, and legal practices. Young people are exposed to extreme viewpoints and encouraged to engage in radical actions. They go to schools that indoctrinate them in hatred for other groups. They learn religious creeds that glorify intolerance. They work in organizations that encourage uncompromising stances. And they operate in legal environments where many people are denied basic liberties.

But extremism has become a growing problem in many societies, including in the West. In large swaths of the United States, for example, moderates have virtually disappeared from the political marketplace. The centrist political leaders who knew how to bargain with and negotiate differences are no longer in power and have been replaced by hardliners on both the left and right who see compromise as a dirty word. This development is the direct cause of the political dysfunction, both in Washington and in many state capitals, that has angered many voters, who then elect even more extremists, thus exacerbating the cycle. The same phenomenon has taken place in a Europe. Nationalist leaders have risen to power, or are threatening to do so, in several places—largely as a consequence of concerns about refugees and immigration. Rather than preach tolerance and multiculturalism, they blame foreigners for deep-seated national problems and thrive on fear and intolerance.

People in these places should not be surprised that their politics have become polarized and extreme. When civil society operates in this manner, it is very likely that politicians will act the same way. *New York Times* columnist David Brooks pointed out in a 2016 column that "the roots of political dysfunction lie deep in society. If there's truly going to be improvement, there has to be improvement in the social context politics is embedded in."[13] It is difficult for elected leaders to act better than those who surround them and, in the case of democracies, judge their behavior at election time.

The crucial question is how to break out of this cycle of extremism, intolerance, and violence. Once civil society allows those perspectives to flourish, it is hard to shift back toward moderation and mutual understanding. Violence begets violence and extremism leads to extremist reactions from others.

Because of their crucial role in perpetuating extremism, leaders need to pay attention to educational and religious organizations within their own countries. They need to evaluate the curriculum and educational viewpoints espoused by teachers. They have to safeguard pedagogic materials to make sure they cover alternative perspectives. Unless civil society eschews radicalism, politics will move away from compromise and negotiation toward extremism and polarization.

CHAPTER 8

Future Possibilities

In looking to the future, it is important to consider prospects for megachange. A number of short- and long-term possibilities have the potential to alter current realities in fundamental ways, among them: Iran developing a nuclear weapon despite its pledge not to do so; robots or other forms of artificial intelligence taking jobs on a widespread scale; rising seas flooding low-lying coastal areas in much of the world; far-right and nationalist forces taking power in parts of Europe and the United States, and damaging both democracy and globalization; and the discovery of primitive life elsewhere in the universe, raising existential questions about religion and humanity itself. Any one of these developments would represent a startling change in the political, social, or religious status quo and create major challenges for political leaders as well as for ordinary people.

Iran Gets a Nuclear Bomb

International concerns that Iran was attempting to develop nuclear weapons heightened in the early 2000s with revelations that the country had built secret research facilities. Starting in late 2006, and accelerating after President Obama entered office, the United Nations imposed global economic sanctions against Iran, intended to force that country to halt its nuclear work. The UN sanctions, backed by an even tougher economic and financial blockade by the United States, were intended to pressure Iran by stopping oil exports, its main source of revenue from overseas.

Despite the sanctions, Iran continued its nuclear research and, by 2015, was using more than 9,000 centrifuges to enrich uranium, a key step in making a nuclear weapon. In theory, those centrifuges could generate enough material for twenty-five nuclear bombs, and some experts believed Iran might be able to develop a weapon in as little as two months.[1]

Eventually, the economic and political pressure, combined with the goals of a reformist government in Iran, led in 2015 to a historic agreement under which Iran pledged to roll back much of its nuclear program. Under this agreement, known as the Joint Comprehensive Plan of Action, Iran agreed to dismantle key nuclear programs, open its facilities to rigorous international inspections, and take other steps intended to prevent it from acquiring a nuclear weapon for at least ten years. Iran's negotiating partners—the United States, four other permanent members of the United Nations Security Council, and the European Union—adopted "snapback" provisions under which sanctions could be reimposed if there were evidence of cheating or noncompliance by Iran.[2]

Even though the agreement was ratified by the relevant parties, critics attacked the agreement for being ineffective and only postponing the inevitable. They argued that the international inspection program was inadequate and it would be impossible to detect whether Iran was upholding its side of the agreement.

The reality is that the agreement could delay but might not permanently stop the alleged Iranian effort to get a nuclear bomb.[3] For example, Iran could respect the international agreement during its ten-to-fifteen-year duration, but develop nuclear weapons after it lapsed. In addition, it publicly could claim to uphold the agreement, but continue its nuclear program in secret and eventually get a bomb. Finally, it could rely on third-party agents outside of Iran to develop a bomb and make materials available at some point in the future.

If Iran eventually develops a nuclear weapon, it would be a major game changer for the Middle East, with broader global implications. The most immediate reaction would come from Israel, which sees Iran as a direct threat because certain Iranian leaders have called for Israel's destruction. A nuclear-armed Iran might threaten an attack or attempt to blackmail Israel; either situation would be extremely dangerous since Israel has its own nuclear weapons.[4]

Faced with a nuclear threat from Iran, Israel might attempt a unilateral bombing attack on Iranian facilities, with the aim of destroying or limiting Iran's nuclear program. Such a raid likely would provoke an Iranian response and therefore risk of a broader regional conflagration.

Israel certainly is not the only Middle Eastern country worried about Iran's nuclear program. Arab states, notably the conservative Gulf monarchies, also would see a nuclear-armed Iran as a potential threat that could destabilize the region and threaten their own regimes. Saudi Arabia, in particular, might well seek to develop its own nuclear weapons, leading to a regional arms race with unpredictable consequences.

All this is in the future, given that Iran has foresworn nuclear weapons for at least a decade. But changed circumstances could lead Iran to backtrack on its promises, or Israel could decide to act preemptively against Iran, or any number of other scenarios could make the always-volatile Middle East an even graver source of instability.

Perhaps an even graver concern is the risk that a terrorist group, such as ISIS or al Qaeda, might somehow acquire a nuclear weapon. Such groups would be more likely than an actual government to use a nuclear weapon, or to threaten its use as a form of blackmail. That kind of development would be very destabilizing for the region and the entire world.

Robots Take the Jobs

The list of new technologies grows every day.[5] Developments as varied as sophisticated robots, augmented reality, machine learning, artificial intelligence, and autonomous vehicles now help people with many different tasks.[6] These technologies are broad-based in their scope and significant in their ability to transform existing businesses and personal lives. In his book *Pax Technica*, political scientist Philip Howard outlines an "empire of bits" that is transforming how people interact with one another.[7]

Robot capacity has increased enormously in recent years and this is likely to have a substantial impact on the future workforce. Figure 8-1 shows the increase in the numbers of industrial robots in operation. In 2013, for example, an estimated 1.2 million robots were in use. This total rose to around 1.5 million in 2014 and is projected to increase to about 1.9 million in 2017.[8] Japan has the largest number with 306,700, followed by North America (237,400), China (182,300), South Korea (175,600), and Germany (175,200). Overall, annual worldwide spending on robotics is expected to rise from $15 billion now to $67 billion by 2025.[9]

FIGURE 8-1. *Industrial Robots around the World, Selected Years*

Millions of robots

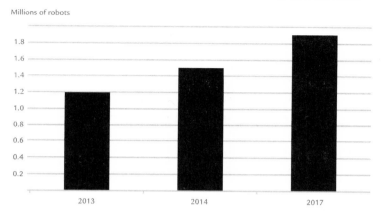

Source: James Hagerty, "Meet the New Generation of Robots for Manufacturing," *Wall Street Journal*, June 2, 2015.

According to an RBC Global Asset Management study, the costs of robots and automation technology have fallen substantially. It used to be that the "high costs of industrial robots restricted their use to a few high-wage industries like the auto industry. However, in recent years, the average costs of robots have fallen, and in a number of key industries in Asia, the cost of robots and the unit costs of low-wage labor are converging. . . . Robots now are a viable alternative to labor."[10]

The Defense Advanced Research Projects Agency held a competition in 2015 for a robot that could perform in hazardous environments. Robots were given eight tasks such as "driving a vehicle, opening a door, operating a portable drill, turning a valve and climbing stairs."[11] The goal was to develop equipment that could operate in damaged nuclear reactors or disaster scenes too dangerous for humans. A Korean team won the competition (with a $2 million first prize) for its robot capable of completing these tasks.

Robots now are able to perform a wide range of programmable social functions. According to a presentation on personal robots, "The early 21st century saw the first wave of companionable social robots. They were small cute pets like AIBO, Pleo, and Paro. As robotics become more sophisticated, thanks largely to the smart phone, a new wave of social robots has started, with humanoids Pepper and Jimmy and the mirror-like Jibo, as well as Geppetto Avatars' software robot, Sophie. A key factor in a robot's ability to be social is whether it can correctly understand and respond to people's speech and the underlying context or emotion."[12]

These devices are handling complex and creative activities. Anthropologist Eitan Wilf of Hebrew University in Jerusalem says that sociable robots represent "a cultural resource for negotiating problems of intentionality."[13] He describes a "jazz-improvising humanoid robot marimba player" that can interpret music context and respond creatively to improvisations on the part of other performers. Designers can put it with a jazz band, and the robot will ad lib seamlessly without listeners being able to discern any difference with human performers.

In the more practical business world, Amazon has organized a "picking challenge" designed to see if robots can "autonomously grab items from a shelf and place them in a tub." The firm currently has around 50,000 people working in its warehouses and it wants to see if robots can perform the tasks of selecting items and moving them around the warehouse. During the competition, a Berlin robot successfully completed ten of the twelve designated tasks. To move goods around the facility, the company already uses 15,000 robots, and it expects to purchase additional ones in the future.[14]

The rapid increase in emerging technologies means there almost certainly will be even greater impact on the workforce than in the past. According to economist Andrew McAfee, "We are facing a time when machines will replace people for most of the jobs in the current economy, and I believe it will come not in the crazy distant future."[15] Technology already is substituting for labor, and the prospect of robots assuming even more responsibility in the workplace has dramatic consequences for jobs and incomes, especially for the middle class.

Martin Ford issues an equally strong warning. In his book *The Lights in the Tunnel*, he argues that "as technology accelerates, machine automation may ultimately penetrate the economy to the extent that wages no longer provide the bulk of consumers with adequate discretionary income and confidence in the future. If this issue is not addressed, the result will be a downward economic spiral."[16]

Continuing, he warns that "at some point in the future —it might be many years or decades from now—machines will be able to do the jobs of a large percentage of the 'average' people in our population, and these people will *not* be able to find new jobs." Firms have discovered that robotics, machine learning, and artificial intelligence can replace humans and improve accuracy, productivity, and efficiency of operations. During the Great Recession, many businesses were forced to downsize their workforces for budgetary reasons. Executives did this in many cases by automating certain functions and using robots or advanced manufacturing techniques to handle tasks formerly done by skilled or unskilled workers.

One way to think about the possible job impact is to study the U.S. Bureau of Labor Statistics (BLS) data on future employment trends. In its most recent analysis, the agency projects that about 9.8 million new positions will be created between 2014 and 2024. This amounts to an overall increase of about 0.5 percent per year in the labor force, which is not a very substantial level of growth.

In looking at particular sectors, health care and social assistance are expected to grow the most with an annual rate of 1.9 percent. This will add around 3.8 million new jobs, representing more than one-third of all the new jobs expected to be created during that period.[17] Other areas that are likely to experience growth include professional services (1.9 million), leisure and hospitality (941,000), construction (790,000), state and local government (756,000), finance (507,000), and education (339,000).

Interestingly, the information sector is one of those expected to shrink in jobs, with the BLS projecting that about 65,000 jobs will be lost there. This is noteworthy because every expert expects technology to revolutionize many businesses, but it will do this by transforming operations, not increasing the number of jobs. Manufacturing is another area thought to lose jobs. The BLS expects that sector to drop 27,000 jobs, while the federal government will shed 383,000 positions, and agriculture, forestry, fishing, and hunting will drop 110,000 jobs.[18]

It is hard to quantify how much the increased use of robots, artificial intelligence, and sensors will affect the workforce because we are in the early stages of the technology revolution. We know that fields such as health care and education have been relatively slow to embrace new technologies. Despite innovations in personalized learning and mobile technology, most K–12 schools still do most of their teaching through traditional means and hire people as the primary agents of instruction. There are more computers and tablets in the classroom, but schools have been unable to scale up innovation to the same degree as some other sectors.

The same problem applies to health care. Hospitals are staffed with people who deliver the bulk of medical treatment. Health providers store information in electronic medical records, and data-sharing networks are connecting lab tests, clinical data, and administration information in order to promote greater efficiency. But old models prevail and there hasn't yet been major disruption in medical care delivery. Both education and health care eventually will undergo disruption, but it may take a while for the full force of technology to alter operations in a significant manner.

In their highly acclaimed book, *The Second Machine Age: Work, Progress, and Prosperity in a Time of Brilliant Technologies*, economists Erik Brynjolfsson and Andrew McAfee argue that technology already is producing major changes in the workforce. The authors say:

> Technological progress is going to leave behind some people, perhaps even a lot of people, as it races ahead. As we'll demonstrate, there's never been a better time to be a worker with special skills or the right education because these people can use technology to create and capture value. However, there's never been a worse time to be a worker with only "ordinary" skills and abilities to offer, because computers, robots, and other digital technologies are acquiring these skills and abilities at an extraordinary rate.[19]

Former U.S. Treasury Secretary Lawrence Summers is equally pessimistic about the future of employment, especially for those lacking higher education and technical skills. He argues that "if current trends continue, it could well be that a generation from now a quarter of middle-aged men will be out of work at any given moment." From his standpoint, "providing enough work" will be the major economic challenge facing the world.[20]

Even more dramatic is Oxford University research that claims technology will transform many sectors of American life. Carl Frey and Michael Osborn studied over 700 occupational groupings and examined the odds of computerization in each field over the next few decades. Their results indicate that "47 percent of U.S. workers have a high probability of seeing their jobs automated over the next 20 years."[21]

Using European data, Economist Intelligence Unit researchers replicated that analysis and found that 54 percent of jobs on the continent are at risk of automation. Looking at the European situation, they concluded that "technology is likely to dramatically reshape labor markets in the long run and to cause reallocations in the types of skills that the workers of tomorrow will need."[22]

Not everyone, of course, agrees with this analysis. Some economists, such as Robert Gordon, predict that technology eventually will create more new jobs than it will destroy.[23] In addition, economics writer Martin Wolf claims that "the impact of these technologies is overhyped."[24] Rather than transforming human existence, he argues that the "pace of economic and social transformation has slowed in recent decades, not accelerated."[25] Digital devices are part of the current milieu, but they do not dictate future realities.

But if current trends continue, robots may well transform the workforce and affect the possibilities for meaningful employment regardless of how many jobs are taken away. The transformation of the economy is likely to alter the manner in which social benefits are delivered. Right now, much of healthcare and pensions are paid for through jobs. People gain credits for retirement by being gainfully employed. However, if a significant part of the future population does not have jobs, society will have to figure out other ways of providing healthcare and making people eligible for a basic income. Failure to do so also will mean that many individuals will not have something meaningful to do with their lives and that these pockets of the unemployed could provide the basis for social or political unrest.

Global Warming and Rising Seas

Almost all leading scientists believe that global warming is real and likely will lead to more frequent and severe storms, alterations in climate patterns across much of the globe, and higher ocean levels as a result of warming water and the melting of ice sheets on Antarctica and Greenland. Mark Fischetti of *Scientific American* writes that "the oceans have warmed, providing more energy for storms. And the Earth's atmosphere has warmed, so it retains more moisture, which is drawn into storms and is then dumped on us."[26]

Researchers are in agreement about rising oceans but unsure at what rate it will take place. Sea levels will rise at different rates around the world, but most forecasts suggest that water could rise above current levels by one to four feet by 2100; some estimates put the overall rise at even higher if ice melting accelerates.[27]

Whatever the exact increase in sea levels, nearly all scientists believe that climate changes will have dramatic consequences for humans. According to Michael Kearney of the University of Maryland, an increase in the sea level is "going to happen to every coastal area around the world, not just here and there."[28] Joshua Willis, an oceanographer at the Jet Propulsion Laboratory, says "people need to be prepared for sea level rise. It's not going to stop."[29] With 2015 being the "second hottest year" since weather records have been kept in 1895, scientists' worry regarding global impact remained quite high.[30]

In recent decades, many people have moved to coastal locations to enjoy the water or be closer to major cities. Some 600 million people around the world reside in poor areas that experience periodic flooding.[31] In the United States, climate experts claim that "40% of the population lives in relatively high population-density coastal areas, where sea level plays a role in flooding, shoreline erosion, and hazards from storms."[32] Areas at risk include some of the globe's most prominent cities: New York City; Boston; Washington, D.C.; San Francisco; Los Angeles; Miami; Madrid; Amsterdam; Venice; Cape Town; Tokyo; Shanghai; Hong Kong; and St. Petersburg, Russia, among others. All of these cities are located on low-lying waterfronts, so a significant increase in sea levels could put parts of them underwater. Businesses and millions of people would be forced to move away from the coast, which would be expensive and disruptive for those communities.[33] Many cities have ports and power plants right on the waterfront, so rising sea levels could endanger energy production and transportation. In this situation, there would have to be massive relocation efforts to save this crucial infrastructure from the rising waters.

A 2016 study estimated that it would cost around $14 trillion to relocate the millions of people in the United States displaced by rising seas. Anything between a three- and six-foot increase would force big changes in business and residential location, according to the researchers. Experts forecast that "coastal Louisiana and the Chesapeake region will see faster rates of change since the land there is also sinking."[34]

The impact of rising seas would be especially devastating for developing countries in Africa and Asia. According to a World Bank study entitled "Turn down the Heat," researchers believe that "poor communities will be the most vulnerable to climate change. . . . [They] cluster in low-lying areas with poor drainage, few public services, and no protection from storm surges, sea-level rise, and flooding."[35]

Governments in coastal areas could build large dikes for water management, similar to what already exists in Amsterdam and Venice. They could develop sophisticated systems to direct water through canals or other waterways to avoid the most populous areas. But such projects would involve considerable costs and infrastructure enhancement. Although it is possible to protect individual neighborhoods through water management, there are no guarantees of being able to do this on a widespread scale around the Earth—and these types of systems are very complex and expensive to maintain.

There also is the question of who pays for personal damages and relocation expenses. Is it the responsibility of the individual or business, or society at large? We are used to dealing with small-scale or temporary environmental dislocations, but not long-term, even permanent flooding on a wide scale. Large-scale change will put enormous financial and political pressure on governments and societies to deliver public benefits.

With weather patterns likely to change even more dramatically than has been the case over the past two decades, meteorologist William Gail believes it will be harder to use the past as a tool to forecast the future. "Nature's longstanding, repeatable patterns—relied on for millenniums by humanity to plan everything from infrastructure to agriculture—are no longer so reliable," he writes. As new trends unfold, there will be a "decline in our ability to predict the future."[36]

Of course, many Americans, including political leaders, still doubt that climate change is real, or say that even if it is real it is a natural phenomenon and is not affected by human behavior, such as burning fossil fuels. Along with generally low levels of scientific literacy among the general public, this lack of understanding complicates the ability of experts to convince leaders and the public of the need to take actions that address this problem.[37] So far it has proven difficult to garner wide public acceptance of actions needed to mitigate climate change before its effects are well advanced. At that point, it will become even more complex and expensive to deal with the consequences.

Finally, there likely will be serious consequences for international politics arising from climate change. Economic deprivation and social unrest often lead to war, refugees, and societal conflict. Nations that lose territory or cropland because of rising seas, sustained drought, and other climate change factors may become more aggressive in dealing with their neighbors. They may seek new territory for their people or areas that can grow food. The prospect of "climate change refugees" already has raised widespread concern because people may have to flee home environments made hostile by higher temperatures, worsening storms, or sea-level rise.[38] This would accelerate mass population migrations at a time when there is little acceptance of refugees crossing national borders.

Even with a global agreement in 2015 by nearly all of the world's nations to limit greenhouse gas emissions, it is not clear when, or even whether, needed steps will be implemented—or how much they will help to ameliorate likely environmental damage. One hundred and ninety-six countries agreed to take some action, which would seem to represent an extraordinary degree of consensus.[39] Yet it is right to worry about whether political leaders, now and well into the future, have the will to reduce emissions in their own countries, especially in the face of economic interests that seek to delay the impact on themselves.

Europe Turns Right and Undermines Democracy

Throughout the post–World War II period, most European nations followed the path of social welfare liberalism that provided generous government benefits and encouraged the notion of "Europe" as a united entity, eventually in the form of the European Union (EU). One of the most important manifestations of this was the opening of internal European borders as a result of the "Schengen Agreement" in 1985; as of 2016 twenty-six European nations allowed citizens of other Schengen nations to cross their borders without passports or visas.[40] Nineteen countries of the twenty-eight EU nations also have adopted the euro as their common currency. Even before these European-wide agreements, former colonial powers such as Britain and France had long accepted migrants from their former colonies. Scandinavian nations have been leaders in accepting political and war-related refugees. Germany has a history of bringing in immigrant guest workers (mainly from Turkey but also other countries) for businesses.

However, concern about terrorism and refugee migration in Europe has shifted the political environment in some of these nations much further to the right. The flood of migrants from North Africa and the Middle East in recent years—particularly in 2015—has sparked a major backlash in several countries and altered national policies. For example, the Netherlands and Norway already have elected governments with strong anti-immigration agendas. In Poland, anti-immigration parties have risen in power even though that country has accepted relatively few refugees. The anti-refugee backlash there helped to elect a conservative government in late 2015 that has reneged on the previous government's pledge to resettle several thousand refugees and has imposed limits on the news media and installed conservative judges on the country's top court.[41]

Macedonia has closed its southern border and Hungary has built a barbed wire barrier to keep out migrants coming from Serbia.[42] Hungary's prime minister, Viktor Orban, says that "all the terrorists are migrants" and uses that argument to justify his tough stances on European migration. He sees his highest priority as "to defend the borders and to control who is coming in." Orban believes that Europeans are at war with Islamists and worries that extremists in the Middle East are sending fighters to Europe in the form of migrants.[43] He specifically cites "rapists and job stealers as justifications for their barriers."[44] Austria, which has hosted tens of thousands of migrants, responded in 2015 by building a fence at its migrant entry point. Public concern about immigration was so high that ultra-nationalist Alexander Van der Bellen came within 30,000 votes (about six-tenths of one percent) of winning the presidency. He campaigned against globalization, free trade, and immigration, and argued his country should seal its borders against the wave of refugees that were sweeping through it.[45]

Germany has witnessed growing popularity by the anti-immigration party known as the Alternative for Germany (AfD). Chancellor Angela Merkel pushed her fellow European leaders in 2015 to accept more refugees but got caught in the domestic backlash when the number entering Germany rose to nearly 1 million. Her own coalition partner in Bavaria disowned her welcoming stance, and the AfD, which had been languishing in the polls, suddenly started rising in popularity.

In 2016 the AfD gained representation in three state legislatures after polling between 13 and 24 percent in elections.[46] Its rallies are attracting thousands of followers, and political observers there worry that "there is a big lurch rightwards" in that country.[47] Meanwhile, Merkel's own poll numbers dropped from 75 to 46 percent between 2015 and 2016, potentially threatening her political survival in the upcoming parliamentary elections.[48] Merkel's finance minister, Wolfgang Schauble, warned that "Europe's open internal borders, known as the Schengen system, faced grave threats and could soon collapse as more countries—including Germany—re-establish border controls and checkpoints to regulate who can enter and leave."[49]

Following the 2015 Paris terrorism attacks, the nativist National Front party in France made major gains in the first round of regional elections, although it did less well in the final elections.[50] Its leader, Marine Le Pen, is a leading contender for the 2017 presidency, depending on whom the mainstream parties nominate. She has criticized President Francois Hollande for "cowardice that made our country vulnerable."[51] She argues that France needs "authentic Frenchness" and an "indispensable cleaning out of the cellars and suburbs gangrened by criminality."[52] For her, that means forcing immigrants, especially Muslims from former French colonies, to assimilate into French culture and society. One commentator predicted that France would become much more conservative in dealing with Muslims, whether native-born or immigrants. "There is a serious risk, in public opinion, that people will become more radical. Maybe people will now say, 'No, no, no Islam in the public space, not anymore,'" noted Bernard Godard, an expert on French-Muslim relationships.[53]

Even Sweden, often considered one of the most liberal and open societies in the world, has imposed new border controls on those entering from Denmark. They must have appropriate travel documents and citizenship status in order to come into that nation. The Danish parliament, meanwhile, passed tough restrictions on migrants, including the government's threat to seize their financial assets greater than $1,500 to help pay for their social benefits. In addition, family members of migrants would have to wait three years before they could apply for reunification with their loved ones.[54]

In the face of terrorist attacks, Europeans have become increasingly open to the idea of governments employing emergency powers against suspected militants.[55] Rather than worrying about privacy and civil liberties, as has been the case in the past, there is new support for additional government monitoring of suspected terrorists.

Some European governments also have taken steps to tighten rules on freedom of expression. Faced with separatist groups in its Basque region, Spain has enacted legislation that outlaws the "glorification of terrorism" and "unauthorized public demonstrations."[56] France has a statute that "punishes statements praising or inciting terrorism." Comedian Dieudonne M'bala M'bala was convicted there for social media statements considered sympathetic to the 2015 *Charlie Hebdo* attack. With fears of terrorism leading legislators to pass restrictive measures, some political commentators worry that "such laws take us on a dangerous slope towards arbitrariness in a democracy."[57]

Increased resistance to European unity—the idea of something similar to a "United States of Europe"—is occurring in parallel with rising fears about immigration. Nationalist and right-wing parties in many countries have balked at what they see as interference by EU bureaucrats in Brussels. This resistance is strongest in the United Kingdom, where many leaders in the ruling Conservative Party long have complained that the economic union has not produced benefits for Britain and even has harmed the country through liberalized international trade. In response to such concerns, Prime Minister David Cameron called a June 2016 vote on withdrawing from the European Union and voters approved the exit. And in France, the conservative National Front party has promised to undertake a public vote on membership in the EU if it wins the 2017 presidential election.[58] These moves threaten not only the very basis of the EU but also the broader concept of globalization itself.

There are signs elsewhere of intolerance and antidemocratic moves in places that have functioning democracies. Turkey has seen its government led by President Recep Tayyip Erdogan shed some of the country's secular leanings and concentrate power in the executive branch. Term-limited as prime minister, Erdogan won election to the presidency, which previously had been a mostly ceremonial office. He then used his leadership of the ruling Justice and Development Party to oust his prime minister, boost his authority over government, and weaken civic institutions.[59] His loyal supporters have attacked major media outlets, undermined the independence of the judiciary, and cracked down on social media and digital news sites, among other things. The government even seized control of the most widely read newspaper, *Zaman*, for criticizing Erdogan's leadership. In 2016 dozens of academics and activists were arrested following protests against government policies.[60] An attempted military coup against him fizzled in a few hours in July 2016.

In India, journalists, politicians, and bloggers have been murdered for expressing secular views that opposed conservative religious practices. The current Indian government has been criticized for playing to Hindu nationalists (its political base) and attacking those who support tolerance. Its culture and tourism minister (Mahesh Sharma) has plans to "cleanse every area of public discourse that had been westernized."[61]

In Bangladesh, prominent publishers have been attacked for criticizing religious extremism. Hit lists of secular writers have circulated among Islamists, and publishers have been warned about promoting blasphemist writers.[62] This has generated considerable worry that this nation is moving away from secular, democratic practices toward an Islamic theocracy.

Even the United States has not been exempt from a resurgence of nativist, anti-immigrant rhetoric. Republican presidential nominee Donald Trump has promised to "build a Mexican-funded wall across the continent, expel 11 million undocumented immigrants, blow up the global trading order, send Syrian refugees back into a war zone, ban the immigration of Muslims to the United States and consider a Muslim registry."[63] Some of his supporters cite these stances as the "politics of the middle finger" in which some voters are anxious to overturn existing policies and institutions, which they believe are not working for them. They praise Trump for "telling it like it is" and don't mind their candidate's use of "contempt, mockery, cruelty, [and] prejudice" as a way to draw attention to these issues.[64]

These difficulties raise the possibility that democratic political systems may become unworkable, at least in some parts of the world. Especially worrisome is the fracturing of traditional political norms. Politicians in many countries routinely attack the news media or use new communications technologies to bypass the press and appeal directly to voters, often with sensationalist claims. It is easy to scare voters during periods of economic anxiety and social disruption. Similar to earlier periods of megachange, such as in the 1930s, many people yearn for strong leaders who they hope will guide them through times of chaos and disorder.

Amidst all these pressures, it is an open question whether democracy can endure in the face of ultra-nationalism, political paralysis, and economic anxiety. Writing twenty-five years ago, political scientist Juan Linz predicted that presidential systems had unhealthy features. He noted that a "fixed presidential term adds a 'winner take all' element to presidential elections, since parties and voters know that they're likely to be stuck with the victor for years. This 'raises the stakes in presidential elections and inevitably exacerbates their attendant tension and polarization.'"[65] His argument appears quite prescient in light of the troubles many contemporary democracies now are facing.

What If We Are Not Alone in the Universe?

Not all threats are political or environmental in nature. Some raise existential questions for human beings themselves. With recent advances in space exploration and scientific knowledge, there is a growing belief among astrophysicists, astronomers, and biologists that microbial life is not limited to planet Earth, and that some forms of primitive life are abundant around the universe. This possibility generates serious questions for religion, philosophy, and even human identity. There are an estimated 200 billion stars in the Milky Way galaxy and there are at least 200 billion galaxies around the known universe.[66] With many stars having multiple planets and moons, quadrillions of objects around the universe might be capable of hosting some type of primitive life.

According to scientists, the necessary components for life as we know it are liquid water, heat, and organic chemicals. The common definition of life is "a self-sustaining chemical system capable of Darwinian evolution."[67] Water is vital because it is a solvent that makes possible many different kinds of chemical interactions. Proteins and amino acids mix well in water and when heated, combine with other elements to form the complex compounds that are the essence of life.[68]

Outside of our solar system, water, heat, and organic chemicals are abundant. "Astronomers see the signature of water in giant molecular clouds between the stars, in disks of material that represent newborn planetary systems, and in the atmospheres of giant planets orbiting other stars," according to a scientist from the National Aeronautics and Space Administration (NASA).[69] Its component elements (hydrogen and oxygen) are very common and have been found on many different kinds of objects around the galaxy, including planets, moons, asteroids, meteorites, comets, and space dust. One NASA astrochemist boldly proclaimed that "if all these molecules that are necessary for life are everywhere out in space, the case gets a lot better that you'll find life outside of Earth."[70]

In our own solar system, scientists have found water and heat sources in many places. Several moons (such as Saturn's Enceladus and Titan, and Jupiter's Ganymede, Callisto, and Europa), asteroids, and comets have water as well as basic molecules. These elements constitute life's building blocks so it is quite plausible to consider the possibility of life beyond our globe.[71]

Some of these celestial objects are believed to have warm oceans under their icy surfaces. Europa, for example, is thought to have a liquid ocean beneath its ice. Gravitational push and pull from Jupiter heats the water and provides a possible energy source. According to scientists, "Europa could provide the possibility not just for life, but, if the conditions were just right, even complex life."[72] Models of its ocean estimate that there is oxygen and hydrogen capable of sustaining microbial life.[73]

Saturn's Enceladus also appears to have a warm ocean underneath its ice. Orbiters have spotted water geysers coming from that moon, and scientists who have studied imaging data have concluded that it "has a huge global ocean below its ice-encrusted surface."[74] Heated by the tidal effect of nearby Saturn plus having hydrothermal activity underground, that moon's water contains salt and organic molecules.[75] Among the compounds detected in Enceladus are "water vapor, carbon dioxide, methane, molecular nitrogen, propane, acetylene, formaldehyde and traces of ammonia."[76]

There is considerable evidence that Mars had liquid oceans in its distant past and still has some flowing water in its steep valleys and craters. "Mars is not the dry, arid planet that we thought of in the past. Under certain circumstances, liquid water has been found on Mars," stated Jim Green, NASA's directory of planetary science.[77] NASA Landers and imaging flybys also have found evidence of water flows and deposits in the sediment. Estimates derived from scientific analysis show that 4.3 billion years ago Mars had 20 million cubic kilometers of water, roughly about the amount of the Atlantic Ocean.[78] Even today, frozen water exists on Mars in the form of polar ice caps.

Around the universe, the Kepler space telescope had found over 3,000 planets in 440 solar systems as of 2016.[79] Some of these bodies fall within a possible habitable zone, being neither too close nor too far from a sun. By measuring changes in light as a planet moves in front of its sun, scientists can estimate the size and mass of each planet. Experts predict that the Milky Way galaxy "has more than 10 billion rocky planets that live in the habitable zones of their stars."[80]

One planet known as Kepler-452b is a possible candidate for life. It is "about 60% larger in diameter than Earth and circles a sun-like star that sits about 1,400 light-years away in the constellation Cygnus. It orbits [its Sun] at roughly the same distance as Earth—its year is 385 days, just 20 days longer than our own—which means it probably gets a similar amount of sunshine."[81]

Since that planet's solar system is around 6 billion years old (older than our own by a billion years), scientists believe this could have been sufficient time for life to evolve. According to Jon Jenkins of NASA's Ames Research Center, "That's considerable time and opportunity for life to arise somewhere on its surface or in its ocean, should all the necessary ingredients and conditions for life exist on this planet."[82]

Leading scientists believe humans are close to being able to document that the conditions for life exist in many places around the universe. For example, Ellen Stofan, NASA's chief scientist, says that "we are going to have strong indications of life beyond Earth in the next decade and definitive evidence in the next 10 to 20 years." Continuing, she noted that "we are not talking about little green men. We are talking about little microbes."[83] Through exploration in our solar system and space telescope analysis of other galaxies, there is accumulating evidence that life is not unique to our planet.

If people on Earth learn that life does exist elsewhere, it will force a dramatic shift in the "Earth-centered" thinking that has dominated human history and remains common today. The news will broaden people's horizons about the nature of the universe, the abundance of life, and the role of religion in human thinking. That discovery would be transformative in terms of how humans see themselves and the worlds around them.

According to Smithsonian Institution astrophysicist Jeremy Drake, the discovery of life elsewhere, whether within our own solar system, the Milky Way galaxy, or the broader universe "would have an enormous impact—psychologically, theologically, socially. . . . Right now, we have a country-wide approach to life—an 'us against them' nationality type of thing. I think if life were detected on other planets, and certainly if communication or signs of civilizations were found, I would hope the perspective would entirely change. We'd become more outward-looking. Would humans feel less self-important? Maybe they would."[84]

Most major religions are centered around the idea of divine intervention on planet Earth. For example, a divinely inspired Muhammad is the central figure in Islam, and Moses and Abraham are key figures in Judaism. If life exists elsewhere, does that mean God sent revered Islamic or Jewish figures to each of those places? Are equivalents of Muhammad, Moses, and Abraham on each planet that has advanced life? Are they the same people as the prophets sent to Earth, or different ones?

The same conundrum applies to Christianity. Most orthodox Christians believe that God sent his son, Jesus Christ, to Earth to die on a cross and save all those who believe in him. If life is abundant around the universe, does that mean that God sent his son to every planet having intelligent life? Did Jesus have to be crucified on every planet with advanced life in order to give its inhabitants a chance at eternal life? If there is intelligent life on other planets, how would a just God provide the possibility of eternal salvation if none of those individuals ever had a chance to learn about Jesus?

One possible answer to the last question is that alien lives are in the same category as human infants who die without being baptized. Church leaders recognize there are many people who die before they "may be saved and brought into eternal happiness" as well as "those who are not yet able to use their reason and freedom" to accept Jesus Christ. According to the International Theological Commission: "There are reasons to hope that God would save these infants precisely because it was not possible to do for them that what would have been most desirable—to baptize them in the faith of the Church and incorporate them visibly into the Body of Christ." Catholic leaders believe that the "mercy of God" may provide "a path to salvation" for these individuals.[85]

Some Catholic theologians, however, claim these discoveries would not affect religious beliefs. "The discovery of intelligent life [on other planets] does not mean there's another Jesus. The incarnation of the son of God is a unique event in the history of humanity, of the Universe. God became a man through Jesus in Palestine 2,000 years ago," said Friar Jose Gabriel Funes, the chief astronomer for the Vatican.[86]

These are just some of the provocative issues that would arise from the paradigm shift caused by knowledge of life elsewhere. There is a possibility that religious faiths would move beyond "earth-based" thinking to more universal perspectives. There also is a chance that religion might fade away in the same way that some cultures gradually lost their strong but implausible beliefs about witch doctors. More likely would be intense reactions and counterreactions at many different levels as people grapple with the meaning of new scientific discoveries.

Dealing with the news that life on Earth is not unique and that there are many places around the universe capable of life could be difficult, even traumatic, for many people not steeped in the latest advances in astronomy. That information would confound popular beliefs and might force a radical reconceptualization of widely accepted religious and philosophical tenets. Over time people would come to understand that their own species, homo sapiens, is not unique in the universe and that their strongly held beliefs about the centrality of humans need rethinking.

Addressing Nightfall

In the science fiction novel *Nightfall,* coauthors Isaac Asimov and Robert Silverberg tell the story of a far-away planet surrounded by six stars.[87] That solar system is so bright, because of the multiple suns, that there is no nighttime on the planet. There also are no visible stars in the sky because people live in constant daylight.

Unbeknownst to the planet's inhabitants, however, once every 2,049 years an eclipse of one of the suns produces a brief nighttime. Since they are not expecting darkness, the people don't know how to deal with such a dramatic change. They have no lights, and for the first time in their recorded memory, the inhabitants of this planet experience nighttime, see other stars, and begin to grasp that their solar system is not the only object that exists.

Sadly, the planet's population cannot cope with this shocking revelation, and according to the writers, many of its inhabitants go insane. Even with the best efforts of its scientists and leaders to prevent mass panic, violence breaks out all over the planet. After great turmoil and suffering, the advanced civilization collapses and much of the technological and scientific progress comes to an abrupt halt. The people simply cannot handle the reality of nightfall and its dramatic ramifications for their conception of themselves and their place in the universe.

While this example may represent an extreme form of existential megachange, this fictional account could be read as carrying warning signs for our contemporary situation. As noted in this volume, numerous megachanges have the potential to transform modern life: vast economic shifts resulting from widespread use of robots and artificial intelligence; political shocks based on the challenges of ethnic tensions and ultra-nationalism; governance failures that spread disease and famine; domestic or international conflict arising from religious extremism; rising seas and natural disasters resulting from climate change; or the dramatic discovery that primitive life exists elsewhere in the universe. Any one of these scenarios could produce tremendous stress and lead to dangerous anxiety, mass migrations, political unrest, or armed aggression.

Now is no time to think small and assume that change will be incremental in nature. Rather, leaders need to think big and accept that change is likely to be fast and substantial. Failure to do this would doom people to wrong-headed remedies and actions that are inadequate for the scope of our challenges.

As noted in previous chapters, a number of steps would help people deal with large-scale transformation. First, recognizing that extremism begets extremism, it is important to deradicalize politics and civil society before intolerance and misunderstanding reach epic proportions. If people learn intolerance at any early age through family life and social institutions, it is difficult to undo those lessons later in life. Reviewing teaching materials and pedagogic lessons is vital to short-circuit political and religious extremism. Unless systems of education, law, and religion create the conditions of peaceful conflict resolution, it will be impossible for political leaders to govern based on those ideals.

Second, to save democracy, there are changes in campaigning and governing that would help people understand the stakes of change and ways to deal with it. It is important to end the winner-take-all system because that mentality elevates the stakes of conflict and makes the losers feel badly about and reject the outcome, whatever it turns out to be. If people feel that one side or one group is earning a disproportionate share of economic and political benefits, political and social conflict are elevated to a high level, with little chance of resolution.

Failed governance has been a particular problem in some Middle Eastern countries. In Iraq, for example, tensions between Sunnis and Shiites have been aggravated by what has been seen by Sunnis as a centralization of oil revenue in a national government dominated by Shiites. Fearing that this economic distribution dooms them to long-term poverty, some Sunnis have fought the central government through both political and military means: problems related to governance and the economy clearly contribute to civil strife.

Third, political institutions in the United States and around the world require reforms to better align policymaking capacity with societal challenges. The processes in many democratic nations were designed for eras of slow change and fewer fundamental challenges. In its infancy, the United States was not a world power and communications took place in terms of days and weeks, not minutes or seconds. With megachange as the new normal, though, alterations in the contemporary era unfold more quickly. Domestic and global processes need to be able to cope with massive economic, political, and social shifts that move quickly around the world.

This means that political systems need to break the veto points that unnecessarily slow decisionmaking. In the U.S. Congress, senators can engage in filibusters (that is, unlimited debate), making it impossible to vote on key appointments or pass pieces of legislation, even if bills have majority support—an example of how certain democratic systems are unable to meet contemporary challenges and resolve major issues.

Fourth, we should extend our conception of change to longer time periods. People need to overcome the "presentism" that syndicated columnist E. J. Dionne bemoans in contemporary politics.[88] One of the reasons people often are surprised is that their civic memory goes back only a few decades, at most. It is vital to consider longer time periods in order to understand that the range of options is much broader and more fundamental than suggested by short time horizons. Putting more emphasis on the teaching of history in school and giving people a greater appreciation of longer-term time horizons would enable people to cope more effectively with large shifts when they happen.

The current generations are not the first to face massive dislocation, technology innovation, refugees, or political paralysis. The twentieth century dealt with two world wars, numerous regional conflicts, totalitarianism, genocide, and extreme poverty. Herculean efforts were required to address those issues and move the world toward postwar peace and prosperity. New international institutions such as the United Nations, World Bank, and International Monetary Fund were created to improve communications and commerce and to enable leaders to resolve contentious disputes.

Some of these global organizations, though, have lost their effectiveness at conflict resolution and problem solving. Just as American institutions need reforms that improve decision-making, bodies such as the United Nations and World Bank should act more forcefully to fight extremism, improve governance, and reduce corruption in public and private sector institutions. Poor governance in many parts of the world weakens confidence in government and makes it difficult to address major policy problems.

Some agencies have appointed chief innovation officers whose jobs are to think big, anticipate major challenges, and develop remedies that address those problems before they arise. We need people in government and elsewhere who think long term, have ideas about how to remake institutions and political processes, and generate solutions for big problems. Otherwise, it will be hard to cope with the complex challenges facing many countries.

In a number of respects, governing capacity has not kept pace with societal challenges. Figuring out how to deal with massive change is one of the biggest issues that humans face. The possibility of local or regional disputes escalating globally is quite substantial and makes it imperative for leaders to improve problem solving and conflict resolution. Finding mechanisms to deradicalize society and lower tensions represent key steps toward resolving these challenges.

Notes

Notes to Chapter 1

E. J. Dionne, "This Time It Really Is the End of Trump. Really," *Washington Post*, April 3, 2016.

1. Elliot Goodman, *The Soviet Design for a World State* (Columbia University Press, 1960).

2. Tim Geithner, *Stress Test: Reflections on the Financial Crises* (New York: Crown Publishing, 2014).

3. Graeme Wood, "What ISIS Really Wants," *The Atlantic*, March 2015.

4. Steven Erlanger, "Britain Votes to Leave E.U.; Cameron Plans to Step Down," *New York Times*, June 23, 2016.

5. Heather Saul, "ISIS Publishes Penal Code Listing Amputation, Crucifixion and Stoning as Punishments," *The Independent*, January 22, 2015.

6. For earlier discussions of this notion, see John Piescik, "Megachange: Leading Change Across Multiple Large Organizations," McLean, Va.: MITRE Center for Enterprise Modernization Technical Report, November 2007; Rob Creekmore, John Piescik, and Nahum Gershon, "Megachange Profiler How-to Guide," McLean, Va.: MITRE, October 2010; and Darrell M. West and Allan Friedman, "Health Information Exchanges and Megachange," Brookings Institution report, February 8, 2012.

7. Alex Tribou and Keith Collins, "This Is How Fast America Changes Its Mind," *Bloomberg Business*, June 26, 2015.

8. Thomas Kuhn, *The Structure of Scientific Revolutions* (University of Chicago Press, 1962).

9. Walter Isaacson, *The Innovators: How a Group of Inventors, Hackers, Geniuses, and Geeks Created the Digital Revolution* (New York: Simon and Schuster, 2014).

10. Jeff Greenfield, "What If Trump Wins?," *Politico Magazine*, August 4, 2015 (www.politico.com/magazine/story/2015/08/trump-wins-2016-gop-nomination-120994).

11. Tyler Cowen, *Average Is Over: Powering America beyond the Age of the Great Stagnation* (New York: Dutton Books, 2013).

12. James K. Galbraith, *The End of Normal: The Great Crisis and the Future of Growth* (New York: Simon and Schuster, 2014).

13. Robert Gordon, *The Rise and Fall of American Growth* (Princeton University Press, 2016).

14. Michael Forsythe, "China Deployed Missiles on Disputed Island, U.S. Says," *New York Times*, February 16, 2016.

15. Jane Perlez, "U.S. Challenges China's Claim of Islands with Sea Operation," *New York Times*, January 31, 2016, p. 8.

16. Jeffrey Bader, "What Does China Really Want," Brookings Institution Order from Chaos blog, February 11, 2016; and Michael Forsythe and Jane Perlez, "South China Sea Buildup Brings Beijing Closer to Realizing Control," *New York Times*, March 8, 2016.

17. Simon Denyer, "Chinese Warnings to U.S. Plane Hint of Rising Stakes over Disputed Islands," *Washington Post*, May 21, 2015.

18. *BBC News*, "Tunisia Suicide Protester Mohammed Bouazizi Dies," January 5, 2011.

19. Kevin Sieff, "They Were Freed from Boko Haram's Rape Camps. But Their Nightmare Isn't Over," *Washington Post*, April 3, 2016.

20. William Wohlforth, "The Stability of a Unipolar World," *International Security*, Volume 24, 1999, pp. 5–41; and Andrew Hurrell, "Hegemony, Liberalism and Global Order," *International Affairs*, Volume 82, 2006, pp. 1–19.

21. Tiffany Howard, *Failed States and the Origins of Violence* (Farnham, UK: Ashgate, 2015).

22. Michael Walzer, *The Paradox of Liberation: Secular Revolutions and Religious Counterrevolutions* (Yale University Press, 2015).

23. Darrell M. West, *Going Mobile: How Wireless Technology Is Reshaping Our Lives* (Brookings Institution Press, 2015).

24. The Brookings Institution Foreign Policy program has a blog called "Order from Chaos: Foreign Policy in a Troubled World."

25. Charles Lindblom, "The Science of 'Muddling Through,'" *Public Administration Review*, 1959; and Aaron Wildavsky, *The Politics of the Budgetary Process* (Boston: Little, Brown, 1979).

26. Jonathan Bendor, "Incrementalism: Dead yet Flourishing," *Public Administration Review* 75, no. 2 (March/April 2015).

27. John Piescik, "Megachange: Leading Change across Multiple Large Organizations" (McLean, Va.: MITRE Center for Enterprise Modernization Technical Report, November 2007); and Rob Creekmore, John Piescik, and Nahum Gershon, "Megachange Profiler How-to Guide" (McLean, Va.: MITRE, October 2010).

28. Keith Poole, "The Polarization of the Congressional Parties," March 21, 2015, at www.voteview.com.

29. Thomas Mann and Norman Ornstein, *It's Even Worse Than It Looks* (New York: Basic Books, 2013).

30. Nelson Schwartz and Quoctung Bui, "Where Jobs Are Squeezed by Chinese Trade, Voters Seek Extremes," *New York Times*, April 25, 2016.

31. Paul Starr, *The Creation of the Media* (New York: Basic Books, 2005).

32. Tiffany Ap, "Al-Shabaab Recruit Video with Trump Excerpt," CNN, January 3, 2016.

33. Ishaan Tharoor, "New Islamic State Video Celebrates Brussels Attacks by Quoting Donald Trump," *Washington Post,* March 24, 2016.

34. Quoted in Mike Allen's Playbook, *Politico*, March 6, 2016.

35. Michela Del Vicario and others, "The Spread of Misinformation Online," *Proceedings of the National Academy of Sciences* (December 4, 2015).

36. Arthur Brooks, "The Real Victims of Victimhood," *New York Times*, December 27, 2015, p. 19.

37. Jacob Hacker and Paul Pierson, "No Cost for Extremism," *The American Prospect* (Spring 2015), p. 73.

38. Timothy Egan, "Hillary's Big Idea," *New York Times*, April 23, 2016, p. A19.

39. *New York Times*, "New Senators Tilt G.O.P. Back toward Government Insiders Vowing to Act," November 16, 2014, p. 22.

40. Paul Schulman, *Large Scale Policy Making* (New York: Praeger, 1981).

41. Randall Roberts, "Grammys 2015: Transcript of Bob Dylan's MusiCares Person of Year Speech," *Pop & Hiss*, February 7, 2015.

Chapter 2

1. James Gleick, *Chaos: Making a New Science* (New York: Vintage, 1987).

2. Edward Lorenz, "Predictability: Does the Flap of a Butterfly's Wings in Brazil Set off a Tornado in Texas?" Address at the 139th Annual Meeting of the American Association for the Advancement of Science, Boston, December 29, 1972.

3. Stephen Kellert, *In the Wake of Chaos: Unpredictable Order in Dynamical Systems* (University of Chicago Press, 1993).

4. Martin Wolf, *Why Globalization Works* (Yale University Press, 2004).

5. Francis Fukuyama, *The End of History and the Last Man* (New York: Free Press, 1992).

6. Matthew Morgan, ed., *The Impact of 9/11 on Politics and War* (New York: Palgrave Macmillan, 2009).

7. *PBS Newshour*, "9/11 to Now: Ways We Have Changed," September 14, 2011.

8. Gallup Poll, "Terrorism in the United States," June 2–7, 2015.

9. Jeffrey Jones, "One in Four Americans Say Lives Permanently Changed by 9/11," Gallup Poll, September 8, 2011.

10. Gallup Poll, "Presidential Approval Ratings, George W. Bush," October 31–November 2, 2008.

11. *Mother Jones*, "How 9/11 Changed the Law," September 9, 2011.

12. *BBC News*, "Tunisia Suicide Protester Mohammed Bouazizi Dies," January 5, 2011.

13. Victoria Carty, "Arab Spring in Tunisia and Egypt: The Impact of New Media on Contemporary Social Movements and Challenges for Social Movement Theory," *International Journal of Contemporary Sociology* 51, no. 1 (April 2014).

14. Andrey Korotayev and others, "The Arab Spring: A Quantitative Analysis," *Arab Studies Quarterly* 36, no. 2 (Spring 2014).

15. Sarah El Deeb and Lee Keath, "Islamist Claims Victory in Egypt Presidential Vote," Associated Press, June 18, 2012.

16. Xinhua, "Egypt's Ousted President Morsi Gets 20 Years in Jail," April 22, 2015.

17. National Public Radio, "Four Years after Revolution, Libya Slides into Chaos," January 31, 2015.

18. Ivan Krastev, "Why Did the 'Twitter Revolutions' Fail," *New York Times*, November 11, 2015.

19. Robin Wright, "How the Arab Spring Became the Arab Cataclysm," *New Yorker*, December 15, 2015 (www.newyorker.com/news/news-desk/arab-spring-became-arab-cataclysm).

20. Mark Urban, "How Many Russians Are Fighting in Ukraine?" BBC, March 10, 2015.

21. Thomas Grove, "Russia Starts Nationwide Show of Force," Reuters, March 16, 2015.

22. William Broad, "In Taking Crimea, Putin Gains a Sea of Fuel Reserves," *New York Times*, May 17, 2014.

23. CNN, "Vladimir Putin's Approval Ratings? Now at Whopping 86%", February 26, 2015; and Michael Birnbaum, "How to Understand Putin's Jaw-Droppingly High Approval Ratings," *Washington Post*, March 6, 2016.

24. Inti Landauro and Noemie Bisserbe, "Charlie Hebdo Attack: Police Actively Searching Area North of Paris," *Wall Street Journal*, January 8, 2015.

25. Sam Schechner, "French Senate Passes Intelligence Bill," *Wall Street Journal*, June 9, 2015; and *The Guardian*, "France Passes New Surveillance Law in Wake of *Charlie Hebdo* Attack," May 5, 2015.

26. Adam Nossiter, "Europe Facing New Uncertainty in Terrorism Fight," *New York Times*, August 23, 2015.

27. Susan Dominus, "The National Front's Post-Charlie Hebdo Moment," *New York Times*, February 18, 2015.

28. Matthew Karnitschnig, William Horobin, and Anton

Troianovski, "A Backlash Swells in Europe after Charlie Hebdo Attack," *Wall Street Journal*, January 8, 2015.

29. Ibid.

30. Adam Nossiter, Aurelien Breeden, and Katrin Bennhold, "Paris Attack Was the Work of 3 Teams, An 'Act of War' by ISIS, France Asserts," *New York Times*, November 15, 2915, p. 1.

31. Griff Witte, Souad Mekhennet, and Michael Birnbaum, "Belgian Authorities Capture Suspect in Brussels Attacks," *Washington Post*, March 23, 2016.

32. Andrew Higgins and Milan Schreurer, "'They Did Not Give Anybody a Chance,'" *New York Times*, November 15, 2015, p. 1.

33. Anthony Faiola, Souad Mekhennet, and Missy Ryan, "French Lawmakers Back Extension of State of Emergency in Anti-Terror 'War,'" *Washington Post*, November 15, 2015, p. 1.

34. Liz Alderman, "Paris Attacks Have Many in France Eager to Join the Fight," *New York Times*, November 26, 2015.

35. Liam Stack, "Poll of British Muslims Reveals Startling Views, but Some Question Methodology," *New York Times*, April 14, 2016.

36. John McCormick, *Understanding the European Union* (New York: Palgrave Macmillan, 2014).

37. *BBC News*, "Greece Debt Crisis," June 30, 2015.

38. Jennifer Rankin, "EU Refugee Crisis: Asylum Seeker Numbers Double to 1.2m in 2015," *The Guardian*, March 4, 2016.

39. Steven Erlanger, "Britain Votes to Leave E.U.; Cameron Plans to Step Down," *New York Times*, June 23, 2016.

40. Michael Birnbaum, "After Brexit, French Right-Wingers Eye Their Own E.U. Exit Hopes," *Washington Post*, June 27, 2016.

41. E. J. Dionne, "This Time It Really is the End of Trump. Really," *Washington Post*, April 3, 2016.

Chapter 3

1. Benjamin Page and Robert Shapiro, *The Rational Public: Fifty Years of Trends in Americans' Policy Preferences* (University of Chicago Press, 1992).

2. United Press International, "Church Defends $10,000 Grant to Angela Davis Defense Fund," May 31, 1971.

3. Angela Davis, *An Autobiography* (New York: Random House, 1974).

4. Bettina Aptheker, *The Morning Breaks: The Trial of Angela Davis* (Cornell University Press, 1997).

5. Alliouagana Garveyite, "Black and Christians in the 21st Century," *Island Mix*, July 23, 2006.

6. Online Christian Colleges, "Megachurch and Megabusiness," undated.

7. Veronique de Rugy, "President Reagan, Champion Budget-Cutter," (Washington: American Enterprise Institute, June 4, 2004).

8. Andrew Glass, "Reagan Declares 'War on Drugs,' October 14, 1982," *Politico*, October 14, 2010.

9. Erik Eckholm, "In a Safer Age, U.S. Rethinks Its 'Tough on Crime' System," *New York Times*, January 13, 2015.

10. Darrell M. West, "How Digital Technology Can Reduce Prison Incarceration Rates," *Newsweek*, April 3, 2015.

11. Cited in Melissa Kearney and Benjamin Harris, "Ten Economic Facts about Crime and Incarceration in the United States," Brookings Hamilton Project, May 2014.

12. U.S. Federal Bureau of Prisons, "Offenses," Washington, D.C., November 28, 2015.

13. Parts of this section are drawn from Darrell M. West, "How Digital Technology Can Reduce Prison Incarceration Rates," Brookings TechTank blog, March 31, 2015.

14. Tracey Kyckelhahn, "State Corrections Expenditures, FY 1982–2010," U.S. Department of Justice Bureau of Justice Statistics, April 30, 2014.

15. Derek Neal and Armin Rick, "The Prison Boom and the Lack of Black Progress after Smith and Welch," Working Paper no. 20283 (Cambridge, Mass.: National Bureau of Economic Research, July 2014).

16. Cited in Melissa Kearney and Benjamin Harris, "Ten Economic Facts about Crime and Incarceration in the United States," Brookings Hamilton Project, May 2014.

17. Darrell M. West, *Billionaires: Reflections on the Upper Crust* (Brookings Institution Press, 2014), pp. 56–57.

18. Ibid.

19. Sam Becker, "7 States Ready to Legalize Marijuana," *Cheat Sheet*, March 28, 2015.

20. Lydia Saad, "Majority Continues to Support Pot Legalization in U.S.," Gallup, November 6, 2014 (www.gallup.com/poll/179195/majority-continues-support-pot-legalization.aspx).

21. Ibid.

22. Philip Wallach and John Hudak, "The Nation Continues to Embrace Marijuana Legalization," *Brookings FixGov Blog*, November 5, 2014.

23. Barbara Brohl, Ron Kammerzell, and Lewis Koski, "Annual Update" (Colorado Department of Revenue, February 27, 2015).

24. Drug Policy Alliance, "Marijuana Legalization in Colorado after One Year of Retail Sales and Two Years of Decriminalization," 2015.

25. Jerry Gray, "House Passes Bar to U.S. Sanction of Gay Marriage," *New York Times*, July 13, 1996.

26. Justin McCarthy, "Same-Sex Marriage Support Reaches New High at 55%," Gallup, May 21, 2014 (www.gallup.com/poll/169640/sex-marriage-support-reaches-new-high.aspx).

27. Ibid.

28. Ibid.

29. Linda Holtzman and Leon Sharpe, *Media Messages: What Film, Television, and Popular Music Teach Us About Race, Class, Gender, and Sexual Orientation* (Armonk, N.Y.: M. E. Sharpe, 2014).

30. *Raw Story*, "'Gay Buying Power' to Hit $2 Trillion by 2012," June 26, 2006 (www.rawstory.com/news/2006/Gay_buying_power_to_hit_1_0626.html).

31. *BBC News*, "How Legal Tide Turned on Same-Sex Marriage in the U.S.," January 16, 2015.

32. Nick Gass, "President Obama on Gay Marriage: Justice Arrived 'Like a Thunderbolt,'" *Politico*, June 26, 2015.

33. Richard Fausset and Alan Blinder, "North Carolina Governor Tries to Step Back from Bias Law," *New York Times*, April 12, 2016.

34. Lawrence Jacobs and Theda Skocpol, *Health Care Reform and American Politics: What Everyone Needs to Know* (Oxford University Press, 2012).

35. Lawrence Jacobs and Theda Skocpol, *Health Care Politics and American Politics* (Oxford University Press, 2012).

36. Theda Skocpol and Vanessa Williamson, *The Tea Party and the Remaking of Republican Conservatism* (Oxford University Press, 2013).

37. Quoted in Darrell M. West, "Republican Big Bucks Backfire," *USA Today*, August 11, 2014.

38. Frank Newport, "Four Years In, GOP Support for Tea Party Down to 41%," Gallup Poll, May 8, 2014.

39. Portions of this section are drawn from Darrell M. West, *Billionaires: Reflections on the Upper Crust* (Brookings Institution Press, 2014).

40. Luisa Kroll, "Inside the 2013 Forbes 400," *Forbes*, September 16, 2013. Also see Arthur Kennickell, "Ponds and Streams: Wealth and Income in the U.S., 1989 to 2007," Federal Reserve Board, January 7, 2009.

41. Marco Cagetti and Mariacristina de Nardi, "Wealth Inequality," *Macroeconomic Dynamics* 12 (2008), p. 285.

42. Thomas Piketty and Emmanuel Saez, "Income Inequality in the United States, 1913–1998," *Quarterly Journal of Economics* 118 (2003), pp. 1–39. For 1999 to 2008 numbers, see the web page of Emmanuel Saez (http://emlab.berkeley.edu/users/saez). Also see Richard Burkhauser and others, "Recent Trends in Top Income Shares in the USA: Reconciling Estimates from March CPS and IRS Tax Return Data," Working Paper 15320 (Cambridge, Mass.: National Bureau of Economic Research, September 2009). Also see Thomas Piketty, *Capital in the Twenty-First Century* (Harvard University Press, 2014).

43. The 2012 income numbers come from Emmanuel Saez, "Striking It Richer: The Evolution of Top Incomes in the United States," unpublished paper, September 3, 2013.

44. Ed Harris and Frank Sammartino, "Trends in the Distribution of Household Income, 1979–2009" (Congressional Budget Office, August 6, 2012).

45. Piketty, *Capital in the Twenty-First Century*.

46. "Selected Measures of Household Income Dispersion: 1967 to 2010," *Current Population Reports* (U.S. Census Bureau, 2011), table A-3.

47. Tami Luhby, "Wealth Inequality between Blacks and Whites Worsens," *CNN Money*, February 27, 2013 (http://money.cnn.com/2013/02/27/news/economy/wealth-whites-blacks/).

48. Jennifer Hochschild, Vesla Weaver, and Traci Burch, *Creating a New Racial Order: How Immigration, Multiracialism, Genomics, and the Young Can Remake Race in America* (Princeton University Press, 2012).

49. Tyler Cowen, "Wealth Taxes: The Future Battleground," *New York Times*, July 21, 2013, p. 6.

50. James Davies and others, "The World Distribution of Household Wealth," Discussion Paper 2008/03 (United Nations World Institute for Development Economics Research, February 2008), p. 7.

51. Branko Milanovic, "Global Inequality and the Global Inequality Extraction Ratio: The Story of the Past Two Centuries" (World Bank, September 2009) (http://elibrary.worldbank.org/doi/book/10.1596/1813-9450-5044). Also see Branko Milanovic, *The Haves and Have-Nots: A Brief and Idiosyncratic History of Global Inequality* (New York: Basic Books, 2012); and Sudhir Arnand and Paul Segal, "What Do We Know about Global Income Inequality?" *Journal of Economic Literature* 46 (March 2008), p. 57.

52. Manuel Funke, Moritz Schularick, and Christoph Trebesch, "Going to Extremes: Politics after Financial Crises, 1870–2014," (Munich, Germany: Center for Economic Studies and Ifo Institute, October 2015), abstract.

53. Norm Ornstein, "The Eight Causes of Trumpism," *The Atlantic*, January 4, 2016. Also see Andrew Prokop, "The Political Scientist Who Saw Trump's Rise Coming," *Vox*, May 6, 2016.

54. Matthew MacWilliams, "The One Weird Trait That Predicts Whether You're a Trump Supporter," *Politico*, January 17, 2016 (www.politico.com/magazine/story/2016/01/donald-trump-2016-authoritarian-213533).

55. Jeff Guo, "A Big Hint about Why So Many People Support Donald Trump Might Come from Germany," *Washington Post*, December 24, 2015 (www.washingtonpost.com/pb/news/wonk/wp/2015/12/24/a-big-hint-about-why-so-many-people-support-donald-trump-might-come-from-germany/).

56. Ezra Klein, "Donald Trump's Ideology of Violence," *Vox*, March 12, 2016.

57. Todd Gitlin, "No One Will Be Able to Stop the Political Violence Donald Trump Is Unleashing," *Washington Post*, March 18, 2016.

58. Robert Kagan, "This Is How Fascism Comes to America,"

Washington Post, May 18, 2016. Also see Peter Baker, "Rise of Trump Tracks Debate over Fascism," *New York Times*, May 29, 2016, p. A1.

59. Michael Crowley, "Will Terror Help Trump?" *Politico*, March 23, 2016, p. 1.

60. Shadi Hamid, "Donald Trump and the Authoritarian Temptation," Markaz blog, Center for Middle East Politics and Policy, Brookings Institution, May 9, 2016.

Chapter 4

1. William Doyle, *The Oxford History of the French Revolution* (Oxford University Press, 2003).

2. Peter McPhee, *Robespierre: A Revolutionary Life* (Yale University Press, 2012).

3. David Garrow, *Bearing the Cross: Martin Luther King Jr. and the Southern Christian Leadership Conference* (New York: William Morrow, 2004).

4. Adam Garfinkle, *Telltale Hearts: The Origins and Impact of the Vietnam Anti-War Movement* (New York: Palgrave Macmillan, 1997).

5. Clark Kerr, *The Great Transformation of Higher Education, 1960–1980* (SUNY Press, 1991).

6. Jane Mansbridge, *Why We Lost the ERA* (University of Chicago Press, 1986).

7. Maurice Isserman and Michael Kazin, *America Divided: The Civil War of the 1960s* (Oxford University Press, 2011).

8. Stephen Prothero, "Why Conservatives Start Culture Wars and Liberals Win Them," *Washington Post*, January 29, 2016.

9. Lee Edwards, *The Conservative Revolution: The Movement That Remade America* (New York: Free Press, 2002).

10. Robert Jones, Daniel Cox, and Juhem Navarro-Rivera, "A Shifting Landscape: A Decade of Change in American Attitudes about Same-Sex Marriage and LGBT Issues," Public Religion Research Institute, February 26, 2014, p. 5 (http://publicreligion.org/site/wp-content/uploads/2014/02/2014.LGBT_REPORT.pdf).

11. Luther Terry, "Smoking and Health: Report of the Advisory Committee of the Surgeon General of the Public Health Service," January 11, 1964.

12. Centers for Disease Control, "History of the Surgeon General's Reports on Smoking and Health," April 8, 2015.

13. Iain Gately, *Tobacco: A Cultural History of How an Exotic Plant Seduced Civilization* (New York: Grove Press, 2007).

14. Julianna Pacheco, "Trends—Public Opinion on Smoking and Anti-Smoking Policies," *Public Opinion* Quarterly 75 (Fall 2011), pp. 576–92.

15. *Bloomberg Businessweek*, "Raise the Smoking Age to 21," November 30, 2015.

16. Gallup, "Tobacco and Smoking," April 8, 2015 (www.gallup.com/poll/1717/Tobacco-Smoking.aspx).

17. Jon Emont, "Antismoking Forces Give Big Tobacco a Fight in Indonesia," *New York Times*, May 1, 2016, p. 12.

18. Judith Johnson, "AIDS Funding for Federal Government Programs: FY1981–FY2009," April 23, 2008, Congressional Research Service, p. 9.

19. Ibid.

20. David Nimmons, "Larry Kramer; AIDS activist; Interview," *Playboy,* September 1993.

21. Kaiser Family Foundation, "HIV/AIDS at 30: A Public Opinion Perspective," June 2011, p. 3.

22. Ibid., p. 8.

23. Roberto deMattei, *The Second Vatican Council: An Unwritten Story* (Fitzwilliam, N.H.: Loreto Publications, 2012).

24. George Weigel, *Witness to Hope: The Biography of John Paul II* (New York: Harper, 2004).

25. Laurie Goodstein, "U.S. Bishops Struggle to Follow Lead of Francis," *New York Times*, November 11, 2014.

26. Jim Yardley and Simon Romero, "Pope's Focus on Poor Revives Scorned Theology," *New York Times*, May 24, 2015, p. 1.

27. Michael Gerson, "Pope Francis Challenges the Faithful," *Washington Post*, November 17, 2014.

28. Laurie Goodstein, "In the Footsteps of Popes Seeking Worldly Change," *New York Times*, June 18, 2015.

29. Somini Sengupta and Jim Yardley, "Pope Francis Addresses U.N., Calling for Environmental Justice," *New York Times*, September 26, 2015, p. A6.

30. Patrick Healy, "Trump Fires Back at Sharp Rebuke by Pope Francis," *New York Times*, February 19, 2016, p. 1.

31. Jim Yardley and Laurie Goodstein, "Francis Signals a Path to Return for the Divorced," *New York Times*, April 9, 2016, p. A1.

32. Michael Gerson, "Pope Francis Challenges the Faithful," *Washington Post*, November 17, 2014.

33. Anthony Faiola, "Conservative Dissent Is Brewing inside the Vatican," *Washington Post*, September 7, 2015.

34. Julie Hirschfeld Davis and Randal Archibold, "Obama Meets Cuban Leader, Making History," *New York Times*, April 12, 2015, p. 1.

35. Gallup, "Attitudes towards Cuba," April 20, 2015 (www.Gallup.com).

36. Walter Kaufmann, *Hegel: A Reinterpretation* (Garden City, N.Y.: Anchor Books, 1966).

Chapter 5

1. Harvey Cox, *The Secular City: Secularization and Urbanization in Theological Perspective* (Princeton University Press, 1965).

2. Conrad Hackett, "The Future of World Religions: Population Growth Projections, 2010–2050," Pew-Templeton Global Religious Futures Project, April 2, 2015.

3. Samuel Huntington, *The Clash of Civilizations* (New York: Simon and Schuster, 1996).

4. Michael Walzer, *The Paradox of Liberation: Secular Revolutions and Religious Counterrevolutions* (Yale University Press, 2015).

5. Michael Paulson, "Aboard Flights, Conflicts over Seat Assignments and Religion," *New York Times*, April 9, 2015.

6. Ibid.

7. Isabel Kershner, "She Was Asked to Switch Seats. Now She's Charging El Al with Sexism," *New York Times*, February 27, 2016, p. A7.

8. *NBC News*, "Jewish Women's Group Defies Rules to Pray at Wailing Wall," October 24, 2014.

9. Steven Erlanger, "Culture Wars Shift in Israel to Art Realm," *New York Times*, January 30, 2016, p. 1.

10. Jeffrey Goldberg, "'Israel Cannot Absorb 3.5 Million Pales-

tinians and Remain a Jewish and Democratic State,'" *The Atlantic*, June 25, 2015.

11. Jewish Virtual Library, "Vital Statistics: Latest Population Statistics for Israel," updated May 2016 (www.jewishvirtuallibrary.org/jsource/Society_&_Culture/newpop.html).

12. Pew Research Center, "Israel's Religiously Divided Society," March 8, 2016.

13. Isabel Kershner, "Israel Cancels Project Barring Palestinians From Some Buses to the West Bank," *New York Times*, May 20, 2015.

14. Ibid.

15. Jodi Rudoren, "Push for Buses on Sabbath Sets off Debate in Israel," *New York Times*, April 25, 2015.

16. Ibid.

17. Yarden Skop, "High School Girls Defy School Ban on Shorts," *Haaretz*, June 1, 2015.

18. Ibid.

19. Ibid.

20. Thomas Friedman, "Netanyahu, Prime Minister of the State of Israel-Palestine," *New York Times*, May 25, 2016.

21. William Booth, "'We Are the Tip of the Spear' That Protects Israel, Radical Settlers Say," *Washington Post*, August 8, 2015.

22. Isabel Kershner, "Israel Continues Crackdown on Jewish Extremist Network in West Bank," *New York Times*, August 9, 2015.

23. Isabel Kershner, "Israel Faces New Brand of Terrorism, This Time from Young Settlers," *New York Times*, January 11, 2016.

24. Mike Ross, "They . . . Do Whatever They Want to Do towards Women Like Me," *Politico*, March 20, 2016.

25. Sayed Salahuddin, "Taliban Ban TV in Afghan Province," Reuters, May 13, 2008.

26. Hashim Shukoor, "Taliban Tries to Stop the Music in Afghanistan—Again," *McClatchy News*, September 3, 2010.

27. William McCants, "The Believer: How an Introvert Became the Leader of the Islamic State," Brookings Institution Essay, September 1, 2015.

28. Graeme Wood, "What ISIS Really Wants," *The Atlantic*, March 2015.

29. Ibid.

30. Rukmini Callimachi, "ISIS Enshrines a Theology of Rape," *New York Times*, August 13, 2015; and Rukmini Callimachi, "ISIS' system of Rape Relies on Birth Control," *New York Times*, March 13, 2016, p. A1.

31. Anna Erelle, *In the Skin of a Jihadist* (New York: Harper Collins, 2015), p. 20.

32. Ibid., p. 33.

33. Lara Rebello, "Seized Documents Point to Daesh Department of 'War Spoils,'" *International Business Times*, December 29, 2015.

34. Karla Adam, "Western Women Are Attracted to Islamic State for Complex Reasons," *Washington Post*, May 28, 2015.

35. Michael Weiss and Hassan Hassan, *ISIS: Inside the Army of Terror* (New York: Regan Arts, 2015).

36. Patrick Cockburn, *The Rise of Islamic State: ISIS and the New Sunni Revolution* (New York: Verso, 2015).

37. Mary Anne Weaver, "Why Do They Go?," *New York Times Magazine*, April 19, 2015, pp. 44–45.

38. Ibid., p. 46.

39. Eliza Griswold, "The Shadow of Death," *New York Times Magazine*, July 26, 2015.

40. Anne Barnard and Hwaida Saad, "ISIS Alternates Stick and Carrot to Control Palmyra," *New York Times*, May 28, 2015.

41. Matthew Rosenberg, Nicholas Kulish, and Steven Myers, "Predatory Islamic State Wrings Money from Those It Rules," *New York Times*, November 30, 2015, p. 1.

42. Ken Miller, *Finding Darwin's God*, Cliff Street Books, 1999.

43. Frank Newport, "In U.S., 42% Believe Creationist View of Human Origins," Gallup, June 2, 2014 (www.gallup.com/poll/170822/believe-creationist-view-human-origins.aspx).

44. Lydia Saad, "One in Four in U.S. Are Solidly Skeptical of Global Warming," Gallup, April 22, 2014 (www.gallup.com/poll/168620/one-four-solidly-skeptical-global-warming.aspx).

45. Lydia Saad, "Three in Four in U.S. Still See the Bible as Word of God," Gallup, June 4, 2014 (www.gallup.com/poll/170834/three-four-bible-word-god.aspx).

46. Frank Newport, "Who Are the Evangelicals?" Gallup, June 24, 2005 (www.gallup.com/poll/17041/Who-Evangelicals.aspx?g_source=evangelical&g_medium=search&g_campaign=tiles).

47. Trip Gabriel and Jonathan Martin, "Republican Field Woos Iowa Evangelical Christians," *New York Times*, April 25, 2015.

48. Summarized in Mike Allen's Playbook, *Politico*, November 23, 2015.

49. Charles Scofield, "Revelation," *Holy Bible* (Oxford University Press, 1967).

50. Jonathan Kirsch, *A History of the End of the World* (New York: Harper One, 2007).

51. William McCants, "How ISIL Out-Terrorized Bin Laden," *Politico*, August 19, 2015.

52. Craig Whitlock and Ellen Nakashima, "For the Islamic State, Paroxysms of Violence Portends Apocalypse," *Washington Post*, November 16, 2015.

53. Graeme Wood, "What ISIS Really Wants," *The Atlantic*, March 2015.

54. Elaine Pagels, *Revelations: Visions, Prophecy, and Politics in the Book of Revelation* (New York: Penguin Books, 2013).

Chapter 6

1. Richard Hamilton, *Who Voted for Hitler?* (Princeton University Press, 1982).

2. Christopher Hilbert, *Mussolini: The Rise and Fall of II Duce* (New York: St. Martin's Press, 2008).

3. Darrell M. West, *Billionaires: Reflections on the Upper Crust* (Brookings Institution Press, 2014).

4. Somini Sengupta, "60 Million People Fleeing Chaotic Lands, U.N. Says," *New York Times*, June 18, 2015. Also see Rod Nordland, "A Mass Migration Crisis, And It May Yet Get Worse," *New York Times*, November 1, 2015, p. 6. UNHCR figures as of December 2015 are at www.unhcr.org/news/latest/2015/12/5672c2576/2015-likely-break-records-forced-displacement-study.html.

5. Somini Sengupta, "Tide of Refugees, but the West Isn't Welcoming," *New York Times*, April 18, 2015, p. 1.

6. Azam Ahmed and Sandra Garcia, "Dominican Plan to Expel Haitians Tests Close Ties," *New York Times*, July 5, 2015, p. A1.

7. Bill Bishop, *The Big Sort: Why the Clustering of Like-Minded Americans Is Tearing Us Apart* (New York: Mariner Books, 2009).

8. Darrell M. West, *Going Mobile: How Wireless Technology Is Reshaping Our Lives* (Brookings Institution Press, 2015).

9. David Rothkopf, *National Insecurity: American Leadership in an Age of Fear* (New York: Public Affairs, 2014).

10. Laila Lalami, "For or Against," *New York Times Magazine*, November 29, 2015, pp. 13–15.

11. Richard Dobbs, James Manyika, and Jonathan Woetzel, *No Ordinary Disruption: The Four Global Forces Breaking All the Trends* (New York: Public Affairs, 2015).

12. William Galston, "Telling Americans to Vote, or Else," *New York Times*, November 5, 2011.

13. International Institute for Democratic Electoral Assistance, "Compulsory Voting," undated (www.idea.int/vt/compulsory_voting.cfm#practicing).

14. William Galston and E. J. Dionne, "The Case for Universal Voting: Why Making Voting a Duty Would Enhance Our Elections and Improve Our Government," Brookings Institution Center for Effective Public Management, September 2015, p. 4.

15. Darrell M. West and Beth Stone, "News Curation vs. Aggregation: Emergence of Editor's Choices Features," Brookings Institution Report, October 2014.

16. Anne Applebaum, "Mark Zuckerberg Should Spend $45 Billion on Undoing Facebook's Damage to Democracies," *Washington Post*, December 11, 2015.

17. Peter Dear, *Revolutionizing the Sciences: European Knowledge and Its Ambitions, 1500–1700* (Princeton University Press, 2001).

18. *National Geographic*, "The War on Science," March 2015.

19. Katherine Noyes, "Vint Cerf Fears a 'Digital Dark Age,' and Your Data Could Be at Risk," *Computer World*, February 13, 2015.

20. "The Story of a Shopping Street in Beijing," *Beijing Review*, December 12, 2013, pp. 34–38.

Chapter 7

1. Cass Sunstein, *The World According to Star Wars* (New York: HarperCollins, 2016).

2. Norman Thrower, *Maps and Civilizations: Cartography in Culture and Society* (University of Chicago Press, 2008).

3. Mark Monmonier, *How to Lie with Maps* (University of Chicago Press, 1996).

4. Merle Ricklefs, *A History of Modern Indonesia since 1300* (London: Macmillan, 1981).

5. Karen Zraick, "Persian (or Arabian) Gulf Is Caught in the Middle of Regional Rivalries," *New York Times*, January 12, 2016.

6. David Eicher, "Asteroid Day," *Astronomy*, July 2015, p. 35.

7. Interfax, "Meteorite-Caused Emergency Situation Regime over in Chelyabinsk," *Russia beyond the Headlines*, March 5, 2013.

8. David Eicher, "Asteroid Day," *Astronomy*, July 2015, p. 35.

9. Elizabeth Kolbert, *The Sixth Extinction* (New York: Picador, 2015).

10. Robert Crease and Alfred Scharff, *The Quantum Moment: How Planck, Bohr, Einstein, and Heisenberg Taught Us to Love Uncertainty* (New York: Norton, 2014).

11. Douglas Brinkley, *36 Days: The Complete Chronicle of the 2000 Presidential Election Crisis* (New York: Times Books, 2001).

12. David Rothkopf, *National Insecurity: American Leadership in an Age of Fear* (New York: Public Affairs, 2014).

13. David Brooks, "How to Fix Politics," *New York Times*, April 12, 2016.

Chapter 8

1. Jess McHugh, "Iran Nuclear Bomb: How Much Nuclear Capacity Does Tehran Already Have?" *International Business Times*, July 14, 2015.

2. Robert Einhorn, "Debating the Iran Nuclear Deal," Brookings Institution, August 2015.

3. Leon Wieseltier, "The Iran Deal and the Rut of History," *Atlantic*, July 27, 2015.

4. Jodi Rudoren, "Israeli Response to Iran Nuclear Deal Could Have Broader Implications," *New York Times*, April 3, 2015.

5. Portions of this section are drawn from Darrell M. West, "What Happens When Robots Take the Jobs," Brookings Institution paper, October 2015.

6. James Manyika and others, "Disruptive Technologies: Ad-

vances That Will Transform Life, Business, and the Global Economy," McKinsey Global Institute, May 2013.

7. Philip Howard, *Pax Technica: How the Internet of Things May Set Us Free or Lock Us Up* (Yale University Press, 2015).

8. James Hagerty, "Meet the New Generation of Robots for Manufacturing," *Wall Street Journal*, June 2, 2015.

9. Alison Sander and Meldon Wolfgang. "The Rise of Robotics." Boston Consulting Group, August 27, 2014 (www.bcgperspectives. com/content/articles/business_unit_strategy_innovation_rise_ of_robotics/).

10. RBC Global Asset Management, "Global Megatrends: Automation in Emerging Markets," 2014.

11. John Markoff, "Korean Team Wins Pentagon's Crisis Robotics Contest," *New York Times*, June 8, 2015.

12. Andra Keay, "The Rise of Social Robots," South by Southwest, March 15, 2015.

13. Eitan Wilf, "Sociable Robots, Jazz Music, and Divination: Contingency as a Cultural Resource for Negotiating Problems of Intentionality," *American Ethnologist*, November 6, 2013, p. 605 (http://onlinelibrary.wiley.com/doi/10.1111/amet.12041/ abstract).

14. Mike Murphy, "Amazon Tests out Robots That Might One Day Replace Warehouse Workers," *Quartz*, June 1, 2015.

15. Dawn Nakagawa, "The Second Machine Age Is Approaching," *Huffington Post*, February 24, 2015.

16. Martin Ford, *The Lights in the Tunnel: Automation, Accelerating Technology, and the Economy of the Future* (2009). Also see his more recent book, *Rise of the Robots: Technology and the Threat of a Jobless Future* (New York: Basic Books, 2015).

17. U.S. Bureau of Labor Statistics, "Employment Projections: 2014-2024 Summary," December 8, 2015 (www.bls.gov/news.release/ecopro.nr0.htm).

18. U.S. Bureau of Labor Statistics, "Employment Projections: 2014-2024 Summary," December 8, 2015 (www.bls.gov/news.release/ecopro.nr0.htm).

19. Erik Brynjolfsson and Andrew McAfee, *The Second Machine Age: Work, Progress, and Prosperity in a Time of Brilliant Technologies* (New York: W. W. Norton, 2014), p. 11.

20. Lawrence Summers, "The Economic Challenge of the Future: Jobs," *Wall Street Journal*, July 7, 2014.

21. Quoted in Harold Meyerson, "Technology and Trade Policy Is Pointing America toward a Job Apocalypse," *Washington Post*, March 26, 2014. For the original paper, see Carl Benedikt Frey and Michael Osborne, "The Future of Employment: How Susceptible Are Jobs to Computerisation," Oxford University, September 17, 2013.

22. Jeremy Bowles, "The Computerisation of European Jobs," Bruegel, July 24, 2014 (http://bruegel.org/2014/07/the-computer isation-of-european-jobs/); and Jeremy Bowles, "Chart of the Week: 54% of EU Jobs at Risk of Computerisation," Bruegel, July 24, 2014.

23. Robert Gordon, *The Rise and Fall of American Growth* (Princeton University Press, 2016).

24. Martin Wolf, "If Robots Divide Us, They Will Conquer," *Financial Times*, February 4, 2014; and Martin Wolf, "Enslave the Robots and Free the Poor," *Financial Times*, February 11, 2014.

25. Martin Wolf, "Same as It Ever Was: Why the Techo-Optimists Are Wrong," *Foreign Affairs*, July/August 2015, pp. 15–22.

26. Paul Barrett, "It's Global Warming, Stupid," *Bloomberg Business*, November 1, 2012.

27. U.S. Environmental Protection Agency, "Increasing Greenhouse Gas Concentrations Will Have Many Effects," undated (www3.epa.gov/climatechange/science/future.html#sealevel). See also Tatiana Schlossberg, "Rising Sea Levels May Disrupt Lives of Millions, Study Says," *New York Times*, March 14, 2016; James Hansen and others, "Ice Melt, Sea Level Rise, and Superstorms," *Atmospheric Chemistry and Physics,* July 23, 2015; Justin Gillis, "Seas Are Rising at Fastest Rate in Last 28 Centuries," *New York Times*, February 22, 2016; Mark Hertsgaard, "Climate Seer James Hansen Issues His Direst Forecast Yet," *Daily Beat* [Daily Beast?], July 20, 2015; and Eric Holthaus, "Earth's Most Famous Climate Scientist Issues Bombshell Sea Level Warning," *Mother Jones*, July 22, 2015.

28. Union of Concerned Scientists, "Preparing for Global Warming's Rising Tides," undated.

29. Matt Hamilton, "Sea Levels Will Rise, Experts Warn, and 'It's Not Going to Stop,'" *Los Angeles Times*, August 27, 2015.

30. Andrew Restuccia, "U.S. Posts Second Hottest Year on

Record," *Politico*, January 7, 2016; and Justin Gillis, "2015 Was Hottest Year in Historical Record, Scientists Say," *New York Times*, January 20, 2016.

31. Carol Matlack, "A Lifeline for Slums," *Bloomberg Businessweek*, September 17, 2015, p. 52.

32. Rebecca Lindsey, "Climate Change: Global Sea Level," National Oceanic and Atmospheric Administration, November 4, 2015.

33. Florida Oceans and Coastal Council, "Climate Change and Sea-Level Rise in Florida," December 2010.

34. Tatiana Schlossberg, "Rising Sea Levels May Disrupt Lives of Millions, Study Says," *New York Times*, March 14, 2016.

35. World Bank, "Turn Down the Heat: Confronting the New Climate Normal," June 19, 2013 (https://openknowledge.worldbank.org/handle/10986/20595).

36. William Gail, "A New Dark Age Looms," *New York Times*, April 19, 2016.

37. Cary Funk and Sara Kehaulani Goo, "A Look at What the Public Knows and Does Not Know about Science," Pew Research Center, September 10, 2015.

38. United Stations High Commissioner for Refugees, "Linking Human Mobility, Disasters and Disaster Risk Reduction," September 2014.

39. United Nations Conference on Climate Change, "Paris Agreement," December 12, 2015 (http://unfccc.int/files/meetings/paris_nov_2015/application/pdf/paris_agreement_english_.pdf).

40. European Commission, "Schengen Area," Migration and Home Affairs (http://unfccc.int/files/meetings/paris_nov_2015/application/pdf/paris_agreement_english_.pdf).

41. Rick Lyman, "Head of Poland's Governing Party Leads a Shift Rightward," *New York Times*, January 11, 2016.

42. Anthony Faiola, "More European Nations Are Barring Their Doors to Migrants," *Washington Post*, January 22, 2016.

43. Matthew Kaminski, "'All the Terrorists Are Migrants,'" *Politico*, November 23, 2015.

44. Peter Coy, "Paris Must Not Lead to Barricades," *Bloomberg Businessweek*, November 29, 2015, p. 12.

45. Alison Smale, "Austrian Far-Right Candidate Norbert Hofer Narrowly Loses Presidential Vote," *New York Times*, May 23, 2016.

46. Geir Moulson, "Nationalists Strong, Setback for Merkel Party in German Vote," *Washington Post*, March 13, 2016.

47. Alison Smale, "Merkel, While Refusing to Halt Migrant Influx, Works to Limit It," *New York Times*, November 29, 2015, p. 6.

48. Roger Cohen, "Will Merkel Pay for Doing the Right Thing?," *New York Times*, February 14, 2016.

49. James Kanter, "German Minister Issues Warning on Open Borders," *New York Times*, January 16, 2016, p. A5.

50. Alissa Rubin, "National Front Gets a Boost in French Regional Elections," *New York Times*, December 7, 2015.

51. Griff Witte, "France's Far Right Reaps Political Gains as Fears of Terrorism Grow," *Washington Post*, November 24, 2015.

52. Adam Nossiter and Liz Alderman, "After Paris Attacks, a Darker Mood toward Islam Emerges in France," *New York Times*, November 16, 2015; and Alissa Rubin, "National Front Gets a Boost in French Regional Elections," *New York Times*, December 7, 2015.

53. Adam Nossiter and Liz Alderman, "After Paris Attacks."

54. Michala Bendixen, "Denmark's Selfish Stance Does Nothing to Help the Global Refugee Crisis," *The Guardian*, January 27, 2016.

55. Andrea Peterson and Brian Fung, "Paris Attacks Should Be 'Wake Up Call' for More Digital Surveillance," *Washington Post*, November 16, 2015.

56. Raphael Minder, "Crackdowns on Free Speech Rise Across a Europe Warry of Terror," *New York Times*, February 24, 2016.

57. Ibid.

58. Ylan Mui, "Why Populist Uprisings Could End a Half-Century of Greater Economic Ties," *Washington Post*, April 18, 2016.

59. Tim Arango and Ceylan Yeginsu, "How Erdogan Ousted Turkish Premier in Drive for Power," *New York Times*, May 6, 2016.

60. Simon Tisdall, "Turkish Opposition Leader Condemns 'Dictator' Erdogan," *The Guardian*, February 15, 2013; and Safak Timur and Tim Arango, "Turkey Seizes Newspaper As Crackdown on Press and Critics Continues," *New York Times*, March 5, 2016, p. A9.

61. Sonia Faleiro, "India's Attack on Free Speech," *New York Times*, October 2, 2015.

62. Ellen Barry, "2 Publishers Stabbed in Bangladesh as Attacks Rise," *New York Times*, November 1, 2015, p. 4.

63. Michael Gerson, "Donald Trump and the Politics of the Middle Finger," *Washington Post*, February 18, 2016.

64. Ibid.

65. Quoted in Charles Lane, "Is U.S. 'Presidentialist' Democracy Failing?," *Washington Post*, February 10, 2016.

66. Caleb Scharf, "Is Earth's Life Unique in the Universe," *Scientific American*, July 15, 2014.

67. Dennis Overbye, "In Icy Breath of Saturn's Moon Enceladus, Cassini Hunts for Life," *New York Times*, October 28, 2015.

68. M. D. Papagiannis, "What Makes a Planet Habitable, and How to Search for Habitable Planets in Other Solar Systems," *Journal of the British Interplanetary Society*, June 1992, pp. 227–230.

69. Preston Dyches and Felicia Chou, "The Solar System and Beyond Is Awash in Water," NASA Jet Propulsion Laboratory, April 7, 2015.

70. Sarah Kaplan, "A Key Ingredient for Life on Earth May Have Crash Landed Here from Space," *Washington Post*, April 8, 2016.

71. Kenneth Chang, "Suddenly, It Seems, Water Is Everywhere in Solar System," *New York Times*, March 12, 2015.

72. John Wenz, "23 Places We've Found Water in Our Solar System," *Popular Mechanics*, March 16, 2015.

73. Preston Dyches, "Europa's Ocean May Have An Earthlike Chemical Balance," Jet Propulsion Laboratory, May 17, 2016.

74. Guneet Bhatia, "NASA Discovers Global Ocean of the Large Water Reservoir in Saturn's Moon 'Enceladus,'" *International Business Times*, September 17, 2015.

75. Wenz, "23 Places We've Found Water in Our Solar System."

76. Dennis Overbye, "In Icy Breath of Saturn's Moon Enceladus, Cassini Hunts for Life," *New York Times*, October 28, 2015.

77. Irene Klotz, "Scientists Find Evidence of Recent Water Flows on Mars," Reuters, September 28, 2015.

78. Karen Northon, "NASA Research Suggests Mars Once Had More Water Than Earth's Arctic Ocean," NASA TV, March 5, 2015.

79. Steve Pond, "Starry, Starry Nights," East Grinstead Online, July 27, 2015, and Adam Frank, "Yes, There Have Been Aliens, *New York Times*, June 10, 2016.

80. Rachel Feltman, "NASA's Kepler Telescope Confirms a Record-Breaking 1,284 New Planets," *Washington Post*, May 10, 2016.

81. Ibid.

82. Amina Khan, "Is Kepler-452b an Earth Twin? More Like a Bigger, Older Cousin," *Los Angeles Times*, July 23, 2015.

83. Abby Phillip, "Why NASA's Top Scientist Is Sure That We'll Find Signs of Alien Life in the Next Decade," *Washington Post*, April 8, 2015.

84. Amy Crawford, "The Search for Life across the Universe," *Smithsonian*, March 12, 2014.

85. International Theological Commission, "The Hope of Salvation for Infants Who Die without Being Baptised," undated (www.vatican.va/roman_curia/congregations/cfaith/cti_documents/rc_con_cfaith_doc_20070419_un-baptised-infants_en.html).

86. Heather Tomlinson, "Alien Life Does Not Undermine the Gospel—Vatican," *Christianity Today*, August 3, 2015.

87. Isaac Asimov and Robert Silverberg, *Nightfall* (New York: Bantam Spectra, 1991).

Index

Index